Cooking from the Heart

Geraldine "Debbie" Troiso

iUniverse books may be ordered through booksellers or by contacting:

iUniverse LLC
1663 Liberty Drive
Bloomington, IN 47403
www.iuniverse.com
1-800-Authors (1-800-288-4677)

Because of the dynamic nature of the Internet, any Web addresses or links contained in this book may have changed since publication and may no longer be valid. The views expressed in this work are solely those of the author and do not necessarily reflect the views of the publisher, and the publisher hereby disclaims any responsibility for them.

ISBN: 978-1-4401-3909-3 (sc)
ISBN: 978-1-4401-3911-6 (hc)
ISBN: 978-1-4401-3910-9 (e)

Library of Congress Control Number: 2009928280

Printed in the United States of America

iUniverse rev. date: 06/12/2014

Dedication

As I grow older and think back, I find all the riches in the world are present in you, my loving family. My heart so filled with love, hugs you within the folds and pages of this book. To my husband Frank and sons Frank and Christopher, for their everlasting love and support. For my "Daughter" Danielle, a special hug and thank you for starting me on the path to this wonderful journey, and to any tiny-blessed addition in my family, this is dedicated to you. You are the butter on my bread, the sugar in my cookies, and the recipe of my life…you are My Life.

Acknowledgments

I would like to propose a toast to thank the many people who helped me bring this book to your table.

First, my sincere thanks to all who shared their favorite recipes with us, answered questions, tasted, tested and always cheered me on. You are all very "Special" to me.

A big debt of gratitude goes to my brother James Pullara and Lewis Hakim, without whom this book could never have become a reality for me. Jimmy built my fantastic website for us to keep this party going. When I accidently deleted the whole site, he rebuilt it with patience and love. Our parents are smiling in heaven for this brotherly love.

Lew put endless hours of work into my computer before I could even begin this exciting journey. They both endured endless questions and telephone calls with unbelievable patience.

My greatest pleasure in this process was working with my niece Francesca Pullara. Fran created my "Cooking from the Heart" logo. I gave her my thoughts, and she took over like a professional and came back to me with an incredible logo that not only came to life but showed what cooking from the heart is all about.

To my cousin Frances Fiorello who gave me my last grammatical editing to perfection.

In addition to the support my husband always gave me to follow a dream, his coming home from work and taking over the typing for me was like an angel from heaven. He is more like a gift from heaven.

There will always be that one person that stands out and leaves an impact on your life. To me this was George Nedeff my Editorial

Consultant. Getting George is probably the closest I'll ever come to winning the New York State lottery. To say thank you just doesn't say enough to show my appreciation. He not only solved my many at the moment catastrophes with calm and patience but he always gave me the encouragement and confidence I needed at times it was overwhelming for me. He truly is priceless and a friend forever.

I have been blessed to count on you my family, friends and advisors and from my heart I thank you all.

Everyone raise your glass and now let's get cooking.

Dear Readers,

Like many Italian families, my mother ruled the kitchen, and never was this more evident than during the holidays. I loved sitting at the table while my mom prepared the Christmas meal, and to me it looked like a tornado passing through the apartment. There were pots and pans everywhere waiting to take the place of the pots and pans already on the stove. The table was overflowing with food waiting to get mixed or popped in the oven. Every space in the kitchen held the beginnings of something delicious or trays of goodies wrapped up for later. It wasn't until our parents passed on and my siblings and I began talking of the "good old days" that I realized I could never remember my mom with a cookbook in front of her, that to me her cooking always came from her heart. It is for this reason I have named my book, Cooking from the Heart, in honor of my mother. I thank my mother for filling my heart with all these great memories and recipes.

This cookbook contains some recipes I learned while growing up in an Italian household and some of my friends that I had to place along with my favorites and so now I'm excited to share them with you.

I'm not a fancy cook who uses exotic spices, though nothing smells better then fresh basil. However, when I can't get fresh herbs, I'm happy to use dried spices, and I can still get a great dish. I have taken many classes at the Culinary Institute of America in Hyde Park New York, and have served as the cook for the priest of my parish at Saint Columba's Church in Hopewell Junction, New York. I have my own business, Homestyle Catering, and at my best when planning parties.

I didn't want to write a book and then leave you on your own. It is my intention to present these recipes to you as if I was there cooking with you, and I'm thrilled to say I will be with you. In this book I have given you my e-mail address and a Web page my brother has made for us. You can always e-mail me to let me know how much you like a recipe or to ask for help with a recipe. On the Web page I'll have all kinds of information for you. Once a month I'll be making a recipe from the book or introducing you to a new one. I will have color pictures of some of the recipes and will offer great ideas for entertaining and much more. I have a guest signing page and please feel free to drop a note to say hi. I also have a great shopping page with Cooking from the Heart gift items. It is my hope to make my book and Web site a fun and new way to cook.

OK!! Let me tell you something about myself. I grew up in an Italian section of Brooklyn NY (you know, the kind of neighborhood where everyone knew your name with someone always watching out the window for all the kids) I went to Saint Joseph Patron School and today I am still in touch with my classmates. I have a close-knit family, with a sister, brother, their spouses and all my wonderful nieces and nephews. I married my childhood sweetheart, (whom by the way, my parents baptized, just to give you an idea how close both sides of our family are) who is the best guy in the world. We have two fantastic sons, and now we have been blessed with a daughter-in-law and always a blessing of many wonderful friends. Can it get any better than this? It truly is a wonderful life. (now you also know my favorite movie)

Remember, I'm just a click away, so let's get to know each other while we cook together-from the heart.

As Always
  Debbie

  debbie#cookfromtheheart.com
  www.cookfromtheheart.com

Contents

In any Italian house, it's all about family and food. No matter what Mommy made, the meal had to start with antipasti. As the years passed, we added new dishes. I can still hear the fun and excitement as we passed the dishes around the table with everyone talking and laughing at the same time. Today this still holds true in my family, and as I think back, I always wondered why Mommy was sitting there with a smile on her face watching us all eat. Isn't it funny how life goes on because, now I'm sitting there with the smile.

When planning on how much to serve, allow 4-6 appetizers per guest if the meal follows quickly, if a late meal is planned allow 6-8 per guest and if it's strictly an appetizer evening plan on 8-10 per guest. A hint Mom gave me was, if you don't have enough leftovers, you didn't make enough, so I always make more than needed.

Appetizers

Cold Antipasti Tray
Easter Meat Pie
Eggplant with Goat Cheese and Balsamic Vinegar
Eggplant Sandwiches
Ginger Chicken
Ham and Cheese Crepes
Homemade Mozzarella
Mozzarella and Anchovy Stuffed Bread
Pepperoni and Mozzarella Muffins
Pork and Provolone Muffins
Homemade Pizza
Rice Balls
Salmon and Cheese Spread Pizza
Stuffed Artichokes
Zucchini Pie

1-lb. block provolone cheese, cut into bite-size pieces
1-lb. block cheddar cheese, cut into bite-size pieces
1-lb. block Swiss cheese, cut into bite-size pieces
8-oz. wheel Brie cheese, cut into bite-size pieces
½ lb. thinly sliced prosciutto
½ lb. thinly sliced salami
½ lb. thinly sliced soppressata (sweet or hot)
½ lb. thinly sliced ham
1 lb. homemade mozzarella (see page 10) or 1 lb. store-bought mozzarella balls
1 small jar or ½ lb. fresh mixed olives
1 jar of roasted red peppers
1 crusty Italian bread or crackers

This is a selection of my family's favorites, but there are so many great cheeses and meats available, you should have no trouble creating a beautiful platter all your own.

To help save space, keep a nice big serving platter next to you as you slice the cheeses and roll the meats. That way you can fill the platter as you work.

First I put the olives and roasted peppers in a pretty dish and place it in the center of the platter (this prevents the oils from mixing into the meats and cheeses).

Then I begin slicing the cheeses into cubes and rolling the meats. Fill the tray with first a cheese and then a meat, to make a separation of your varieties. Continue alternating this way until everything is surrounding the olives and peppers.

Serve with crackers or slices of crusty bread.

Serves 10

'Easter Meat Pie

I first had meat pie at a friend's house when I was a young girl. I loved it so much, that I asked for the recipe and brought it to Aunt Rose to make it for our next holiday. Nowadays, we can't celebrate a holiday without this dish. This makes a nice big tray, so we always have leftovers. Whether you serve this dish warm or cold, you're going to love it. Enjoy!

Dough

3 cups flour
1 ½ cups vegetable shortening, melted and cooled
3 eggs, beaten
6 tbs. sugar
7–9 tbs. water

Filling

1 lb. thinly sliced prosciutto
2 sticks dry sausage (Soppressata 12-oz. pkg.) skin removed and cut into circles
1 lb. mozzarella, sliced thin
1 basket of wet cheese or basket cheese, drained overnight and sliced thin (this can be purchased at a Italian delicatessen)
2 lbs. of ricotta with 2 beaten eggs added
4 hard-boiled eggs, sliced in circles

Preheat oven to 350°.

In a large bowl add flour, cooled shortening, eggs, and sugar. Start with 5 tbs. of water, and add more as you mix if dough is too dry.

With fingertips spread pieces of dough over the bottom and up the sides of an ungreased 11 × 16 inch pan. (Be sure to save some dough to make strips to cover top.)

After I make my dough, I set myself up by getting all my filling ingredients ready.

Layer your ingredients starting with prosciutto. Using the back of a spoon spread approximately one-third of the ricotta evenly over the prosciutto, next your sliced eggs (saving half for one other layer). Place half of the basket cheese over the eggs with the rest also for one more layer. Next is one-third of the dry sausage, ending your first layer with mozzarella. Continue with your next layer until you have used all your ingredients.

Now with extra dough, make strips and crisscross the top. Beat an egg yolk and 1 tbs. water together (egg wash), and brush on top of pie. Bake approximately 45 minutes or until crust is a beautiful golden brown. Don't over bake or it will be dry. Cut into 2-inch squares when ready to serve.

Serves about 30

Eggplant with Goat Cheese and Balsamic Vinegar

2 large eggplants, peeled and sliced lengthwise in ½ inch slices
2 pkgs. Goat cheese, ½ inch thick slices
2 cups balsamic vinegar, reduced
2 tbs. sugar
Oil for frying

To reduce vinegar, pour 2 cups balsamic vinegar and sugar in medium pot. Bring to a boil, reduce heat to a simmer and let boil down to half the amount (consistency should be syrupy)

Preheat oven to 375 °

Fry your eggplant slices in a skillet over medium high heat until a nice golden color (about 4-5 minutes on each side) remove and lay on a paper towel covered dish to soak up excess oil as you continue to fry the rest of slices.

Place a slice of cooked eggplant on a dish lengthwise, place a piece of goat cheese on top. Roll up and place in your baking dish with seam side down. Continue until all your eggplant slices are filled and rolled. Bake uncovered 20 to 30 minutes or until bubbly

For presentation, place some outside lettuce leaves on a serving platter and lay your eggplants rolls on top. Drizzle with reduced balsamic vinegar and serve.

Serves 6 guests with 2 eggplant rolls per person.

Eggplant Sandwiches

We first had this at Aunt Sue's house. I ate so many I couldn't eat any dinner and wouldn't leave that night without the recipe.

> 1 large eggplant, cut in ½-in. thick circles and dusted with flour
> 1 lb. shredded mozzarella
> ½ cup grated Romano cheese
> 1 tsp. fresh or dried parsley
> 2 beaten eggs, 1 for filling and 1 for dipping
> 2 cups seasoned bread crumbs (more as needed)
> Oil for frying

After you dust the eggplant, lightly fry in oil; drain well on paper towels.

To prepare filling, put mozzarella, grated cheese, parsley, and 1 egg in a bowl and mix together.

Lay 1 eggplant circle flat and put some mixture in center and spread a little but not to edge. Cover with another eggplant slice to make a sandwich. In a medium bowl beat the remaining egg and dip the eggplant sandwich to coat all sides and then into the bread crumbs.

When all the sandwiches are breaded, fry in oil over medium-high heat until golden brown. Place fried eggplant on paper towels to remove excess oil.

Serves 8

Ginger Chicken

This recipe is a big favorite of ours that I got many years ago at a party. We serve this as a cold appetizer, but we have shared this with friends who now make it once a week for dinner as a hot dish. Make this the day before if you are serving cold.

> 5 lbs. boneless chicken breast, cleaned, patted dry, and cut into bite-size pieces
> 3 eggs, beaten
> 3 cups of bread crumbs, salt to taste
> ¾ cup soy sauce
> ¾ cup sugar
> 1 piece of fresh ginger (about the size of your thumb) grated
> Oil for frying

Stir soy sauce, sugar, and ginger together really well till sugar is dissolved and set aside.

Dip chicken in egg and then into salted plain bread crumbs; fry over medium-high heat until fully cooked to a nice brown color (about 3 minutes on each side).

Put chicken in a bowl that has a tight cover. Pour the soy sauce mixture over chicken; cover, shake, and refrigerate. Every few hours turn it over and shake again.

Serves 15 as a cold appetizer

Ham and Cheese Crepes

Crepes

> 3 eggs
> 1 cup flour
> 1 cup milk
> ½ tsp. salt

Filling

> 1 cup sour cream
> 6 green onions (scallions) sliced
> ½ tsp. Dijon mustard
> ½ tsp. salt
> pepper to taste
> 3 cups shredded cheddar cheese
> 1 ¼ lb. thinly sliced ham
> ½ cup melted butter
> ⅔ cup bread crumbs

In a blender or with a hand mixer, blend eggs, flour, milk, and salt for 1 minute. Scrape sides of bowl or blender and blend another 30 seconds, cover and refrigerate for 2 hours, this allows the flour particles time to swell and soften, which makes for crepes that are light in texture.

Using a nonstick 8-inch pan (I use a little cooking spray for the first few crepes then it'll be fine) heat your pan to hot but not smoking. Pour 2 tbs. of batter in pan and tilt the pan in all directions so batter covers pan in a thin film. Cook about 1 minute or till a light color appears then flip over to color other side. Remove from pan and place on a tray to cool.

In a bowl, mix the first four filling ingredients. Spread 1 tbs. of mixture in center of each crepe but not to edge. Sprinkle with cheddar cheese, place a slice of ham on top, and roll up.

Lay crepes seam side down in a 15 x 9 inch ungreased pan. Brush with a little melted butter and sprinkle bread crumbs on top. Bake for 12 minutes at 350 degrees.

Makes about 16 crepes

Homemade Mozzarella

Making this cheese was one of the main reasons I wanted to go to the Culinary Institute. My family loves cheese, and it has always been so exciting for me to be able to put something on the table that I've made. Just read the instructions a few times and you'll see it's a piece of cake to make. I have included a few versions so you can see how simple it is to be creative with flavors as well.

You can find cow's milk curd either in a good delicatessen or at a dairy farm. My brand is Polly-O, and it comes in a 42-lb. carton. We make 3-lb. packages and freeze it until we need it. This way it's always on hand when we have a craving.

In a large, deep pot bring very hot tap water to a temperature of 110° over medium heat. Once temperature is steady, add 7 oz. of salt and stir to dissolve.

Break the 3-lb. piece of curd in two (working with one half at a time makes the process easier) and put one portion into the pot and let it sit a few minutes until it starts getting soft and stringy. Using a large spoon (I use a wooden spoon), start lifting it up to stretch it. Put it back in water and pull it up again, keep doing this till cheese is soft smooth and glossy.

Have a two-foot piece of plastic wrap ready. When the cheese is glossy, lift it out of water, and using your hands, form it into a ball. (It's best if you do this near the sink so you can have the cold water running to cool your hands if needed.) Place cheese on the plastic wrap and roll it up so that you have a long piece of wrap on either side of the ball to hold onto. Grasp the two ends and spin the cheese to make it come to a tight ball, tie the two ends together to make a knot and refrigerate till set, about 1 hour.

Presentation

I slice the cheese and place on a round platter. You can add sliced tomatoes in between each slice and sprinkle with chopped fresh basil and olive oil. You can also add thinly sliced onions in between the cheese and tomatoes and sprinkle balsamic vinegar on it. Slice some great Italian bread and you're set.

Variation 1

Prepare the cheese as instructed, but instead of forming into a ball spread the cheese onto a long piece of plastic wrap to about a ¼-inch thick rectangle and top with 1 lb. of thinly sliced prosciutto. Roll it like a jelly roll cake from the shorter side, making sure to roll it very tight, and then place the log on another long piece of plastic and roll it up. Holding the two ends, continue to roll on counter to make it a tighter roll. You can't tie the ends so I use scotch tape to keep it closed. Refrigerate for about 2 hours until set. When ready, remove the plastic wrap, but first cut the two ends off then gently roll off the plastic wrap, using a serrated knife, slice into ½-inch circles and place on a serving platter. Serves about 30.

Variation 2

After you have spread cheese into a rectangle, top with pesto (see page 181) and proceed the same way.

Please try this because it reads harder to make than it really is and you'll love the results. The only thing you have to be careful of is not to get the water too hot. If you do the cheese will dissolve. Just add cold water if you see it's steaming.

Mozzarella and Anchovy Stuffed Bread

    1 loaf Italian bread
    1 2-oz. can anchovy fillets
    1 lb. fresh mozzarella or store bought sliced

Preheat oven to 375°.

Slice the bread on an angle, but do not cut it all the way through.

Spread the bread open and place a slice of cheese and a piece of anchovy into each opening. Pour the oil from the can of anchovies on the bread and cover in foil wrap, closing tightly.

Bake for about 15 to 20 minutes. Serve the whole bread on a platter so your guests can pull off pieces as needed.

Pepperoni and Mozzarella Muffins

1 pkg. of frozen bread dough (contains 3 1-lb. loaves) The night before I plan to make these, I put 2 tbs. of oil in a very large bowl or pot, add the bread dough, cover it with plastic wrap, and let it rise overnight. The next day I punch dough down and cut it in half. I use the other half to make the version that follows this one.
1 lb. thinly sliced pepperoni circles
1 lb. cubed or shredded mozzarella
2 muffin tins, very lightly sprayed with cooking spray (The pepperoni has oil in it so only a light coat is needed.)

Preheat oven to 375°.

On a floured surface, roll the dough into a rectangle; place pepperoni on dough (leave the edges free) and sprinkle with cheese.

Start rolling from short side making a tight roll. Halfway through, cut straight across, leaving the rest for the next roll.

Cut each roll into 12 pieces and place in muffin tin flat side down pressing dough to make it spread to fill cup, there is no need to have the dough rise a second time

Bake 20 minutes or until the dough is a nice golden color and cheese has melted.

Pork and Provolone Muffins

The bread dough left over from the pepperoni muffins
1 lb. ground pork (uncooked)
1 ½ lbs. of provolone cut into small cubes
2 muffin tins sprayed with cooking spray

Preheat oven to 375°.

On a floured surface, roll the dough into a rectangle. Spread the meat evenly and then top with cheese and a little pepper (I lightly press on it to push the meat and cheese into the dough).

Start on short side and roll up making a tight roll. Halfway through, cut straight across leaving the rest for your next roll.

Cut each roll into 12 slices and place in muffin tin flat side down, pressing dough to make it spread to fill cup. There is no need to have the dough rise a second time.

Bake for 25 minutes or until golden brown and pork has no pink color.

These are so delicious you'll want them at every party.

Homemade Pizza

This recipe is from my ninety-four-year-old Aunt Rose.

Dough

>   5 lbs. flour
>   2 oz. yeast with 1 tsp. sugar mixed in 8 oz. warm water and set aside to bloom
>   64 oz. water
>   ¼ cup oil
>   2 oz. salt

Sauce

>   4 1-lb. 12-oz. cans of your favorite crushed tomatoes
>   1 large onion, chopped fine
>   1 tbs. oregano (I crush it in my palms as I'm putting into sauce to give it a finer texture.)
>   salt and pepper to taste
>
>   4 lbs. mozzarella

In a large bowl, add 3 cups of the flour. Add the water, salt, oil and the bloomed yeast and mix well. Continue to add flour until it all comes together. Turn the dough out on the surface and add remaining flour and knead dough until texture is smooth and elastic. In a large bowl (add a little oil just to coat the bowl), place dough and cover with plastic wrap and keep in a warm place until it doubles in size (approximately 2 hours).

While the dough rises, fry onion in a large deep pot till slightly golden; add tomatoes and spices, and cook about 45 minutes at a medium boil (do not add any water).

Preheat oven to 375°.

When dough is ready, grease pans with vegetable shortening. Cut off 1-lb. pieces of dough and spread them in your pans.

Let sit 30 minutes before adding toppings. You can either put cheese on first and cover with sauce, or sauce first and then cheese; it's your preference. Add any other toppings your family likes and bake for 25 minutes on the middle rack in oven. Check the bottom of the pizza for signs of doneness (it should be a beautiful golden brown). We always use kitchen shears to cut homemade pizza—a hint from Aunt Rose.

Rice Balls

Aunt Rose was the rice ball maker and I remember standing next to her waiting for her to give me a rice ball before all the company came. Over the years I have fooled around with it, and my recipe has been in restaurants and Italian delicatessens. You'll really love this one.

> 2 lbs. uncooked rice
> 2 eggs, beaten
> 1 cup grated Romano cheese
> 1 lb. shredded mozzarella
> salt to taste
> 2 beaten eggs with a ½ cup water (egg wash)
> plain bread crumbs (add salt and pepper to taste)

In a large, deep pot, rinse the rice off a little (just to get some of the starch off). Discard that water and add fresh to fill the pot three-quarters of the way full. Cook for 22 minutes and strain rice.

Put the rice in a large bowl or back in pot and immediately add the 2 beaten eggs. Stir with a fork (a fork is best because it won't mash your rice) to coat all the rice; add 1 tbs. salt (or to taste), mozzarella, and grated cheese, and mix well.

If using a deep fryer, fill to indicator line and preheat your oil to a temperature of 375°. If using a deep pot on stove, fill with 4 inches of oil and bring to the same temperature.

In a bowl beat 2 eggs and ½ cup water, and in another, mix your bread crumbs with desired quantity of salt and pepper.

Take the amount of rice you can fit in a ½-cup measure and make it into a ball. Dip the ball in the egg wash and then roll it in the bread crumbs. Set aside and continue until all rice balls are made.

Whether using a fryer or a deep pot make sure not to over crowd the rice balls. Cook the rice balls until they are a deep golden brown. When cooked remove and place on a wire rack to drain and set.

Makes about 40 rice balls

Here is another version I make: Along with cheeses, add ¼ lb. of chopped prosciutto to the rice mixture. To the bread crumbs, add ¼ tsp. of rosemary garlic seasoning (I picked this up at Sam's Club). If you can't find this spice, you can use plain rosemary, and if you're not a fan of rosemary, you can eliminate the spice and still have great flavor from the prosciutto.

Salmon and Cheese Spread Pizza

1 store-bought partially cooked pizza crust, baked (I use Boboli crust.)
a little olive oil and pepper to taste
¾ lb. thinly sliced smoked salmon
8 oz. pkg. cream cheese, softened
½ cup of shallots chopped
¼ cup drained capers
2 tbs. dried dill
1 tbs. lemon juice (I use bottled, but if your preference is fresh, by all means use it.)

Preheat oven to 450°.

Rub some oil on the pizza crust and sprinkle with pepper; bake for 10 minutes. (I put it right on middle rack of the oven without a pan.)

In a medium bowl, add the cream cheese, shallots, 2 tbs. capers, 1 tbs. dried dill, and lemon juice, and mix till smooth and creamy.

Spread the mixture on the crust and top with the salmon (I kind of curl it to look like a rose). Add a few more capers and sprinkle a little more dill. Cut it into wedges or squares, and serve on pizza board for a cute effect.

Stuffed Artichokes

This can be served as a single appetizer or a side dish.

    4 artichokes
    3 cups plain bread crumbs
    4 cloves chopped garlic
    ½ cup grated Romano cheese
    salt and pepper to taste
    olive oil

Wash your artichokes and, with scissors, snip off all the tips. Then cut the bottoms off to make a flat surface to sit in pot.

In a bowl combine bread crumbs, garlic, grated cheese, salt, pepper and blend together. Add just enough oil to make a coarse (but not oily) mixture.

Hold artichoke over the bowl and spread the leaves open; with your hand, fill the cavities of the leaves with the mixture (I love it filled full).

Place each filled artichoke in a large pot and add water to cover almost halfway up artichoke; drizzle a little more oil just on the top of the crumbs.

Cook covered on medium boil. Depending on size, artichokes should take about 1 hour to cook. Keep checking to see that the water has not boiled down; if needed, just add some more water.

Artichokes are cooked when a leaf can be pulled off easily.

Zucchini Pie

This is a great-tasting way to get the family asking for seconds on vegetables.

>   1 medium onion, diced
>   4 zucchini, peeled and diced
>   4 eggs
>   1 ½ cup all-purpose baking mix (I use a brand called Bisquick.)
>   ½ cup oil
>   1 cup grated Romano cheese

Preheat oven to 350°.

In a bowl, combine all ingredients and mix well; pour into a greased 11 × 7 inch baking dish and bake for 45 minutes. Cut into squares and serve.

Serves 20

Soups

Chicken Soup
Creamy Corn Chowder
Hearty Vegetable Soup
New England Clam Chowder
Onion Soup
Pea Soup
Seafood Chowder
Stocks

There is nothing like a hot bowl of soup before dinner. If soup is not intended as the main course, count on 1 quart per six guests; as a main course, plan on 1 quart to serve two.

Chicken Soup

1 whole chicken (about 4 lbs.) or chicken parts
2 large onions
3 stalks celery
4 carrots
salt and pepper to taste
1 lb. of soup pasta

Wash chicken and put in a deep 3-quart pot. Add peeled onions, celery, and carrots, and add water to cover ¾ of all ingredients.

Cook 1 ½ to 2 hours at a low to medium boil; remove the chicken and set aside,

Place the carrots in a bowl; mash them and set aside. Take out onions and celery, and discard the celery. Strain the chicken soup into another pot and then add the mashed carrots and the onions back into the soup pot.

Remove the chicken from the bones (discard the skin and bones) and cut half the chicken into small pieces, adding that to your chicken broth. Save the rest for chicken salad or even better make my Chicken Pot Pie (see page 57).

Cook your pasta kind of on the al dente side; strain and pour into your soup pot. My family recommends using lots of grated cheese to top your soups.

Creamy Corn Chowder

3 slices bacon
1 large onion, chopped
1 lb. small red potatoes, peeled and cubed
2 ½ cups chicken broth
6 large ears corn, or 2 pkg. (10 oz. each) frozen corn
18 saltine crackers, crumbled
2 ½ cups milk
½ tsp. salt
¼–½ tsp. red hot pepper sauce (optional)
1 tbs. minced parsley

Cook bacon in large, heavy nonstick saucepan over medium-high heat until crisp. Transfer to paper towels and when cooled, crumble and set aside. Sauté onion in pan drippings until soft, about 5 minutes. Stir in potatoes and broth and bring to a boil. Reduce heat to medium and simmer until your potatoes are tender, about 20 minutes.

If using fresh ears of corn, stand cobs upright and cut off kernels with a serrated knife (you need 3 cups). If using frozen corn, put kernels in colander and rinse with warm water; drain.

Put cracker crumbs into a medium bowl; stir in milk and let stand until crackers are soft, about 5 minutes.

Meanwhile, use an immersion blender to puree about half of the potato mixture while still in saucepan on stove. Or, transfer half of potato mixture to food processor and puree; return to saucepan. Stir in cracker mixture, corn, salt, and red pepper sauce. Cook until flavors have blended, about 10 minutes. Ladle soup into bowls and top with bacon and parsley.

Serve with extra crackers or crisp bread.

4 celery stalks, diced
5 carrots, peeled and diced
16 oz. fresh mushrooms, sliced
½ small cabbage, chopped (any variety of cabbage)
2 medium onions diced
1 15 oz. can of chickpeas (garbanzo), liquid included
1 15 oz. can of red chili beans, liquid included
1 15 oz. can of white beans, liquid included
⅔ cup of sugar
⅔ cup vegetable oil
1 cup marinara sauce, store-bought, your own, or from recipe
on page 95
6 cups chicken stock

In a pot large enough to hold all the ingredients, heat the oil over medium-high heat.

When oil begins to ripple, add the onions and sugar; stir to coat. Cook stirring often until the onions begin to turn light brown, about 5 to 10 minutes.

Add the rest of the ingredients except for the marinara sauce and stock. Cook stirring occasionally for an additional 5 minutes.

Add the marinara sauce and cook another 5 minutes, stirring often. Add the stock and bring to a boil; lower the temperature until you have a gentle boil.

Cook partially covered for 1 hour or until the carrots are soft.

Makes 8 large hearty servings

We've made this soup with many different vegetables and have found that these flavors best compliment each other. To make a more-filling soup, we also serve it in bowls with noodles.

New England Clam Chowder

½ cup celery, diced small
½ cup onions, diced small
½ cup butter or margarine
½ cup flour
24 oz. clam juice
12 oz. can of chopped clams with juice
1 qt. milk
¼ tsp. salt
⅛ tsp. white pepper
2 cups potatoes cut into small cubes

In a 4-quart saucepan, melt butter or margarine; add celery and onions, and sauté about 5 minutes or until tender.

Add flour and stir continuously for a few minutes so as not to burn the flour; stir in the clam juice, chopped clams, and milk, and bring to a boil. Reduce heat and add potatoes. Season with salt and pepper; when potatoes are cooked, soup is ready to enjoy. Serve with crackers.

Onion Soup

This is better than any onion soup we've had in a restaurant. Let me know if you agree.

    6 medium onions sliced lengthwise
    4 tbs. butter
    5 cups beef bouillon broth
    3 to 4 tsp. Worcestershire sauce
    ½ tsp. salt
    1 tsp. paprika
    6 slices French bread, toasted
    ½ cup grated Romano cheese
    6 slices of mozzarella cheese

Preheat oven to 400°.

Cook onions in butter until a straw color, about 10 minutes.

Add bouillon broth, Worcestershire sauce, salt, and paprika, and cook till onions are tender, about 20 minutes.

Pour soup into oven-safe bowls, place a slice of toasted bread on top, sprinkle grated cheese on the bread, and place a slice of mozzarella on top.

Bake for 10 minutes or till cheese has melted.

Pea Soup

1 large onion, chopped
4 large carrots, chopped into small cubes
5 stalks of celery, chopped small
1 1-lb. bag green split peas, washed, and drained
ham bone (sometimes I'll use a ham steak)
10 cups of water
½ tsp. pepper
4 medium potatoes cut into bite-size pieces
4 tbs. oil to sauté vegetables

In a deep pot, heat oil and sauté onions, carrots and celery until starting to get tender. Add the washed split peas, ham bone, water, and pepper, and cook over medium heat for 25 minutes; reduce to low for 45 minutes.

Take ham bone out of pot. Pull all the meat off and put it into the soup. Add the potatoes at this time and cook till tender.

Total cooking time is 2 ½ hours. Stir occasionally to blend the peas into the liquid. Serve with croutons or Italian bread and butter.

2 8-oz. bottles clam juice or 2 cups homemade fish stock (see
page 33)
4 bacon slices, minced
6 raw shrimp, peeled and deveined
6 scallops
3 pieces of salmon fillet cut into bite-size pieces (Partially
freezing the salmon will make it easier to cut.)
1 large onion, diced
3 tbs. all-purpose flour
1 bay leaf
½ tsp. fresh thyme leaves, chopped
1 lb. potatoes, peeled and diced
3 cups heavy cream or half-and-half
6 tbs. dry sherry (or to taste)
salt and pepper (to taste)
Tabasco sauce (to taste)
Worcestershire sauce (to taste)

Cook the bacon slowly in a soup pot over medium heat until lightly
crisp, about 8 minutes.

Add the onion and cook, stirring occasionally, until the onion is
translucent, about 5–7 minutes.

Add the flour and cook over low heat, stirring with a wooden spoon,
for 2 to 3 minutes.

Whisk in the first bottle of clam juice or stock. Bring to a simmer
and cook for 5 minutes, stirring occasionally. The liquid should be
the consistency of heavy cream. If it is too thick, add more clam
juice or stock to adjust the consistency. Add the bay leaf and fresh
thyme.

Add the potatoes and simmer until tender, about 15 minutes.

When the potatoes are tender, add the shrimp, scallops, salmon, and the cream, and cook another 15 minutes on medium heat.

Stir in the sherry, and season to taste with salt, pepper, Tabasco, and Worcestershire sauce.

Serve in bowls with crackers on the side.

While canned stock saves time and does the job, there is nothing like homemade stock.

Chicken Stock

Make sure you rinse the chicken bones well and use a slotted spoon to remove any scum that collects as the stock cooks.

1 tbs. oil
1 large onion, peeled, halved, and sliced
1 carrot, peeled and halved
1 celery stalk, halved including leaves
1 whole head of garlic with the skin, cut in half horizontally
4 bay leaves
½ tsp. dried basil
½ tsp. dried thyme
½ tsp. dried tarragon
½ tsp. dried oregano
2 lbs. raw chicken bones, including carcass, wings, necks, and feet (no skin or fat)
½ tsp. whole black peppercorns
1 tbs. salt
4 qt. water

Heat oil in a large stockpot over high heat; add the onions, carrots, celery; and garlic, and sauté, stirring occasionally, for 2 to 3 minutes.

Add the remaining ingredients and bring to a boil. Skim off the cloudy scum that comes to the top, but try to avoid removing the peppercorns.

Reduce heat to low and simmer uncovered for 2 hours.

Skim the surface and strain through a fine sieve. Discard the bones and vegetables. Allow stock to cool completely and then refrigerate overnight.

The next day, remove any congealed fat from the surface. Freeze the stock in 1- or 2-cup containers (you can even freeze in ice cube trays). Keeps for 1 month

Brown Chicken Stock

Brown chicken stock is richer in taste and darker in color than the basic chicken stock. For this recipe you use the same ingredients and cook it the same way as the basic chicken stock, but you also add 1 or 2 large tomatoes, coarsely chopped. Place the bones in a pan and drizzle them lightly with oil, and roast at 425° for 15 minutes before adding them to the stockpot.

Beef, lamb, and veal stocks can be made by following the same directions as those given for brown stock; just substitute beef, lamb, or veal bones.

Fish Stock

If you are friendly with your local fishmonger, he may save the trimmings for you.

> 8 cups fresh raw fish bones, including heads and carcasses from fish such as cod, pollock, grouper, snapper, or flounder (Do not use bones from oily fish such as bluefish or mackerel.)
> 4 qt. water
> 2 onions, peeled, halved and sliced
> 2 carrots, peeled and chopped
> 2 celery stalks, chopped
> 2 lemons, halved
> 8 bay leaves
> ½ cup chopped fresh parsley
> 1 tsp. dried basil
> 1 tsp. dried tarragon
> 1 tsp. dried oregano
> ¾ tsp. whole black peppercorns
> 2 tsp. salt

Place fish bones in a large pot with enough water to cover. Bring to a boil over high heat. Remove from heat and drain off the water through a colander.

Rinse the bones thoroughly under cold water. Place them back in the pot with the remaining ingredients and 4 quarts of fresh water. Bring to a boil again over high heat.

Reduce heat to low and simmer for 10 minutes. Turn the heat up to medium and continue cooking for 30 minutes. Allow to cool for 10 minutes.

Strain and refrigerate or freeze in 1- or 2-cup containers or in ice cube trays. Keeps for one month

Breads

Banana Bread
Cheddar Apple Bread
Easter Bread
English Muffin Bread
Irish Soda Bread
Onion Bread
Popovers
Zucchini Bread

Banana Bread

¾ cup sugar
6 tbs. (¾ stick) margarine or butter, softened
2 large eggs
1 cup mashed bananas (about 2 ripe large bananas)
¼ cup water
2 cups all-purpose flour
¾ tsp. baking soda
½ tsp. salt
½ cup walnuts, chopped

Preheat oven to 350°. Grease and flour a 9x5 inch loaf pan.

In a large bowl with mixer at low speed, beat sugar, margarine or butter, and eggs just until blended.

Increase speed to high; beat until light and fluffy, about 5 minutes.

Reduce speed to low and add mashed bananas and ¼ cup water; beat until well mixed.

Add flour, baking soda, and salt, and beat just until blended, constantly scraping bowl with rubber spatula. Fold in nuts; spoon batter into loaf pan and smooth top evenly.

Bake 50 to 55 minutes or until toothpick inserted in center of bread comes out clean. Cool bread in pan on wire rack 10 minutes. Remove from pan and cool completely on rack.

Makes 12 servings

Cheddar Apple Bread

2 ½ cups flour
¾ cup sugar
2 tsp. baking powder
½ tsp. cinnamon
2 eggs, beaten
¾ cup milk
⅓ cup butter or margarine, softened
2 cups sharp cheddar cheese shredded
1 ½ cups peeled, chopped apples
¾ cup chopped nuts
½ tsp. salt

Preheat oven to 350°.

Combine dry ingredients. Add combined eggs, milk, and margarine or butter; mix well. Stir in remaining ingredients and spoon into well-greased and floured 9 × 5 inch loaf pan. Bake for 65 to 70 minutes or until a toothpick inserted in center comes out clean. Let stand 5 minutes then remove from pan.

Serves 12

Easter Bread

The first time I had this bread I knew it was a keeper. It is so moist, and the anise extract gives it a lovely aroma and flavor. We just spread a little butter on a slice and it's heavenly.

2 ½ pkgs. dry yeast
1 cup warm water
1 dozen eggs
1 cup oil
11 cups flour
2 cups sugar
anise extract (1-oz. bottle)
2 beaten egg yolks

Dissolve the yeast in warm water and set aside until frothy.

In large bowl, mix flour and sugar and set aside

Beat eggs in another bowl; add oil and anise, and mix well. Add yeast and stir. Make a well in center of flour bowl and slowly add liquids, stirring to bring it all together. When blended, turn dough out on table top and knead until smooth and elastic, about 7 minutes. (Use flour on hands if sticky.)

Place dough in a well-greased large bowl and cover with plastic wrap and set in a warm place and let rise overnight.

The next day, preheat oven to 350°.

Cut dough into 4 pieces and either shape each loaf in a braid or smooth top and place in a greased loaf pan (no need for a second rise) bake for 45 minutes. When bread comes out of oven, brush with the egg yolk and let dry.

Serves 12

Tell me if this isn't the best Easter Bread you have ever tasted.

English Muffin Bread

This bread tastes just like real English muffins but without the nooks and crannies. Just slice, toast, and spread with jam or butter.

    2 pkgs. dry yeast
    6 cups flour
    1 tbs. sugar
    2 cups milk
    ¼ tsp. baking soda
    ½ cup water
    cornmeal
    2 tsp. salt

Preheat oven to 400°.

Combine 3 cups flour, yeast, sugar, salt, and baking soda in a large bowl.

Heat all the liquids until very warm; add to the flour bowl and mix well. Stir in rest of flour to make a stiff batter.

Spoon evenly into two loaf pans that have been greased and sprinkled with cornmeal on bottom and up sides. Sprinkle cornmeal on top of loaves and cover; let rise in a warm place for 45 minutes.

Bake for 25 minutes. Remove from pan and cool. Slice and toast as needed.

Irish Soda Bread

Every year for St. Patrick's Day, my Irish girlfriend would send us a loaf of her Irish soda bread. It was so delicious. We use to count the days until it was here. I always sent her a green gift for her day (like filling my cream puffs with green cream) to make her feel special.

4 cups flour
3 tbs. sugar
1 tbs. double active baking powder
1 tsp. salt
¾ tsp. baking soda
6 tbs. butter, softened
1 ½ cups dark seedless raisins
1 tbs. caraway seeds
2 eggs
1 ½ cups buttermilk

Preheat oven to 350°.

Grease a 2-quart round baking dish.

In a large bowl, mix first five ingredients with fork. With a pastry blender or two knives, cut in butter until mixture resembles coarse crumbs; stir in raisins and caraway seeds.

In a small bowl, beat the eggs slightly with fork; remove 1 tbs. and reserve. Stir buttermilk and remaining egg into the flour mixture just until the flour is moistened. The dough will be sticky.

Turn out on a well-floured surface; with floured hands, knead dough about 10 strokes or until mixed thoroughly.

Shape dough into a ball and place in casserole dish. In the center of the ball with a sharp knife cut a 4-inch cross about ¼-inch deep. Brush dough with the reserved egg.

Bake for 1 hour and 20 minutes or until a toothpick inserted comes out clean. Cool in pan on wire rack for 10 minutes. Remove from pan and continue to cool completely on rack.

Serves 12

Onion Bread

2 large onions, sliced in rings
3 tbs. butter
2 cups all-purpose baking mix (I use Bisquick brand.)
1 egg
¾ cup milk
1 cup sour cream
½ tsp. salt

Preheat oven to 375°.

Melt butter in skillet and fry onions till golden brown; set aside.

In a bowl, add all other ingredients and stir. (If too thick, just add a little more milk.)

Grease an 8x8 square baking dish, spread mixture evenly and lay fried onions on top of mixture. Bake for 30 minutes, after it has cooled cut into squares.

Serves 12

Popovers

2 eggs, slightly beaten
1 cup milk
1 cup flour
¼ tsp. salt

Preheat oven to 425°.

Grease your popover pan with vegetable shortening or cooking spray and place in heated oven for one minute so that it's hot when you pour your batter into it. (If you don't have a popover pan, you can use a regular muffin pan, but your popovers won't get as high.)

With a blender or hand mixer, beat all ingredients till light and frothy. Fill hot pan three-quarters full with batter and bake for 35 to 40 minutes.

Serves 6 if cooked in a popover pan or 12 in a muffin pan

These are the best. I think you'll love them.

Zucchini Bread

2 cups grated zucchini
4 eggs
½ cup grated Romano cheese
1 cup all-purpose baking mix (I use Bisquick brand.)
½ cup vegetable oil
1 tsp. dried parsley
1 small (8 oz.) mozzarella cut in small cubes
1 clove garlic, chopped fine
pepper to taste

Mix all ingredients, pour in a greased 5 × 8 inch loaf pan, and bake in a 350° preheated oven.

When baking in a glass pan, reduce temperature by 25°.

Bake 55 minutes

Salads

Coleslaw
Potato Salad
Spinach and Strawberry Salad

Coleslaw

My mom always made this the day before because it got softer from the cooked onions and was creamier. This always was a favorite of the family, and I know it'll also become one of yours.

> 1 large cabbage, cored
> 1 ½ large onions, sliced thin
> 4 tbs. butter
> 1 cup mayonnaise (to start)
> salt and white pepper to taste
> 1 tbs. white vinegar

Melt butter in sauté pan; add onions and cook till translucent and tender (but no color).

Chop the cabbage in very thin slices. In a bowl, stir together the cabbage and onions; add the vinegar, salt, and pepper. Stir in the mayo, adding more until mixture is creamy.

Potato Salad

5 lbs. potatoes
1 qt. jar mayonnaise
1 medium onion, chopped fine
3 stalks celery, chopped fine
¼ cup white vinegar
¼ cup milk
salt and white pepper to taste

Boil potatoes. Peel and cut cooled potatoes into cubes.

In a bowl, add mayo, milk, vinegar, salt, and pepper, and blend it really well to a creamy consistency. Add the onions and celery and stir. Add the cubed potatoes and mix well.

I'm always asked to bring this to any party we have.

Spinach and Strawberry Salad

My niece Karen brought this dish to a baby shower, and instead of looking at the gifts, we were all copying this recipe.

1 24oz. bag of baby spinach
4 pints strawberries, cleaned and cut into slices
1 cup of vegetable oil
1 cup of sugar
½ cup white vinegar
¼ tsp. dry mustard
1 tbs. dried minced onions
¼ cup sesame seeds
¼ cup poppy seeds
1 tsp. paprika
1 tsp. Worcestershire sauce

In a blender, add oil, sugar, vinegar, dry mustard, minced onions, sesame and poppy seeds, paprika and Worcestershire sauce and blend until it thickens.

In a large serving bowl, add the spinach and strawberries, just before serving add the mixture over the salad and mix well.

Main Dishes

Chicken a la King
Chicken with Black Olives
Chicken Cacciatore
Chicken with Onions
Chicken Parmigiana
Chicken with Prosciutto
Chicken or Turkey Pot Pie
Chicken Valdostana with Mushroom Sauce
Pork Wellington
Pot Roast
Pulled Pork Roast
Sausage and Peppers
Stuffed Cabbage
Roasted Turkey
Shrimp Parmigiana
Shrimp Scampi
Sole with Crab Stuffing
Stuffed Peppers
Veal Marsala
Veal Parmigiana

Generally, red meat should reach an internal temperature of 160°; poultry, 180°; and pork, 150°–160° before serving. If preparing fish, the surface of the fish should flake off with a fork.

Thaw all meat in the refrigerator for maximum safety.

When I make chicken dishes, I generally use boneless, skinless breasts, but any dish can be made with chicken parts. Actually, the dish is tastier when cooked with the bone in, but it's just a preference thing.

Chicken a la King

I make this dish whenever we have leftover chicken or turkey.

> Your leftover cooked chicken or turkey, cut into bit-size pieces
> 2 tbs. butter
> 2 tbs. flour
> 2 cups milk
> 1 small jar of pimentos, diced
> salt and pepper to taste

In a pot, make a roux by first melting the butter over medium heat and then adding the flour, stirring to blend it well. Using the back of a spoon, mash the mixture to make a paste; stir another minute to cook the raw flour off (be careful not to burn it). Slowly add the milk, stirring constantly to let the flour soak into the milk after each addition.

Add your cut meat, pimentos, salt, and pepper, and cook at a low boil until sauce is creamy and thick.

This goes great with popovers (see page 43). You can fill them with the chicken, or make rice as a side dish and serve with a popover on the side.

Chicken with Black Olives

4 split chicken breasts, bone in, skin removed
2 medium onions, diced
1 8-oz. can small black pitted olives
1 15-oz. can crushed tomatoes
1 10-oz. pkg. sliced mushrooms
6 tbs. oil for frying

In a deep frying pan over medium-high heat, add 6 tbs. oil and cook the breasts until golden brown on both sides. Remove the chicken and place them in a deep dish to catch the juices.

In the same frying pan, add the onions and sauté until they are soft. Return the chicken to the pan along with any juices, and then add the olives, mushrooms, and crushed tomatoes. Stir and spoon the tomato mixture over the chicken breasts. Reduce heat and cover; simmer for another hour.

Serves 4

This is great served over cooked rice.

Chicken Cacciatore

Every Italian household has a version of this dish. It was always a favorite of my mother's because everything went into one baking dish; it was also one of mine because there were less dishes to wash.

> 4 medium chicken breasts washed (it's your preference for boneless or skinless)
> 4 large potatoes, peeled and sliced into steak fries (lengthwise)
> 1 15-oz. can of peas
> 1 14.5-oz. can of tomato sauce
> 1 tsp. oregano
> salt and pepper to taste
> 1 cup water

Preheat oven to 350°.

Place chicken in a 9 × 13 inch baking dish. Put the sliced potatoes all around and in between the pieces; sprinkle with salt, pepper, and oregano. Add the water to the bottom of the pan.

Bake for 45 minutes uncovered, add the peas and the tomato sauce and continue cooking 30 minutes longer or until the potatoes are tender.

Serves 4

Chicken with Onions

6 boneless, skinless chicken breasts (approximately 3-4 lbs.)
washed and patted dried
1 stick butter
2 large onions, chopped
2 cups plain bread crumbs
2 tbs. flour
salt and pepper to taste
2 eggs, beaten
6 tbs. oil for frying

Preheat oven to 350°.

Add the flour, salt, and pepper to the bread crumbs and mix well.

Dip chicken first into the beaten eggs and then the bread crumb mixture. To a frying pan over medium-high heat, add 6 tbs. oil and cook chicken until it is light golden in color. Remove chicken and place in a 9 × 13 inch baking dish.

Melt butter in the frying pan and sauté onions until they start to turn a slight tan color.

Place the onions over the chicken. Cover with foil and bake for 45 minutes. Remove foil and cook an additional 15 minutes.

Serves 6

Chicken Parmigiana

4 boneless, skinless chicken breasts, rinsed and patted dried
2 cups plain bread crumbs
1 medium onion, chopped
1 29-oz. can crushed tomatoes
3 tbs. sugar
1 can of water using the empty tomato can
¼ cup grated Romano cheese
1 tbs. dried parsley
1 tsp. dried oregano
2 eggs, beaten
salt and pepper to taste
1 lb. mozzarella cheese, sliced, shredded, or cubed
Oil for frying

Parmigiana Sauce

In a medium pot, lightly brown onion; add crushed tomatoes, sugar, water, salt, pepper, and oregano, and cook at a low boil for 25 minutes.

Preheat oven to 375°.

Mix bread crumbs, grated cheese, parsley, salt, and pepper in a bowl. Dip chicken first in beaten eggs and then into bread crumb mixture; fry over medium-high heat until golden brown, about 2 minutes on each side.

Spoon some sauce in a 9 × 13 inch baking dish (just enough to cover bottom). Lay the chicken on top of the sauce and then spread mozzarella cheese on top. Sprinkle with the grated cheese and add another layer of the tomato sauce.

Bake uncovered for 45 minutes or till chicken is tender.

Serves 4

Chicken with Prosciutto

4 boneless, skinless chicken breasts
4 thinly sliced pieces of prosciutto
1 cup heavy cream
½ cup Madeira wine

Preheat oven to 350°.

Heat 4 tbs. of oil in a frying pan over medium-high heat; add the chicken, and cook until lightly browned on both sides.

While the chicken is cooking, mix the wine with the heavy cream and blend well.

Place browned chicken in a 9 × 13 inch baking dish.

Place a slice of prosciutto on each breast and then pour the wine mixture over the chicken. Bake uncovered for 20 to 25 minutes.

Serves 4

Chicken or Turkey Pot Pie

Any time we have leftover chicken or turkey, I make a pot pie.

Using your leftover chicken or turkey, cut into bite-size pieces
1 onion diced
3 carrots, peeled and sliced
3 potatoes, peeled, diced and set aside in cold water
1 8-oz. pkg. frozen cut string beans
1 16-oz. jar of store-bought chicken or turkey gravy; also add any homemade leftover gravy or water if needed
2 tbs. oil for frying
2 cups all-purpose baking mix (I use Bisquick.)
1 cup milk
salt and pepper to taste

Preheat oven to 400°.

In a large, deep pot, heat oil over medium-high heat and fry onions until they begin to turn light golden. Add the carrots, string beans, store-bought and leftover gravy, add some water to just about cover vegetables if needed and cook over low heat until the vegetables are almost cooked. Add the potatoes; when almost done, add the chicken or turkey, and cook another 15 minutes.

In a bowl, add the all-purpose baking mix to milk and stir. Pour the chicken or turkey stew into a baking pan and spoon the mixture on top; spread evenly.

Bake for 30 minutes or until the crust is golden brown

Chicken Valdostana with Mushroom Sauce

6 boneless chicken breast, pounded to ¼ inch thickness
10 mushrooms, thinly sliced
6 thin slices prosciutto
6 slices fontina cheese
1 cup dry white wine
1 cup veal or bold beef stock
2 tbs. flour
8 oz. butter
1 tbs. chopped fresh parsley
pepper to taste
2 tbs. cornstarch mixed with 4 oz. cold water
Gravy Master seasoning and browning sauce

Lightly flour chicken, shaking off excess flour

In a large skillet over low heat, melt 6 oz. butter and lightly brown chicken about 2 minutes on each side. Remove and set aside.

Increase heat to medium and add mushrooms, sauté until juices are rendered, about 4 minutes. Add wine and simmer for 3 to 4 minutes to reduce. Increase heat to high, add stock, parsley, pepper and simmer until sauce is reduced to 1 cup, about 10 minutes.

Mix the cold water and cornstarch, add it into your sauce until it thickens, add the seasoning and browning sauce, enough to make a deep brown color. Add 2 tbs. butter and swirl around until melted and sauce is shiny.

Top each piece of chicken with a slice of prosciutto and a slice of the cheese, return to sauce skillet and cook until the cheese has melted.

Transfer chicken to serving platter and pour mushroom sauce on top and serve.

Pork Wellington

1 ½ lb. fillet of pork
salt and pepper
stuffing as described below
1 ½ sheets of puff pastry
6 oz. lean ham, thinly sliced
1 beaten egg

Stuffing

1 small package of mushrooms, finely chopped
1 onion finely chopped
4 tbs. butter
salt and black pepper to taste
1 tsp. powdered thyme
2 tbs. chopped parsley, fresh or dried
4 tbs. plain bread crumbs
2 eggs, well beaten

Preheat oven to 375°.

Preparing the Stuffing

Sauté finely chopped mushrooms and onion in the butter; season to taste with salt, pepper, and thyme. Add parsley and bread crumbs. Stir in beaten eggs and mix well; heat through. Turn out onto a small pan and set aside to cool.

Preparing the Pork Fillet

Season fillet lightly with salt and freshly ground black pepper; sear it quickly over high heat until brown on all sides.

Roll puff pastry into a rectangle of about a ¼-inch thickness. Place fillet in center of pastry; spread evenly with stuffing and top with thin slices of ham.

Fold one side of pastry over the pork. Brush a little beaten egg over the upper surface and then fold over the second side of the pastry, overlapping the first. Roll pastry ends out flat; brush with beaten egg on the upper side and fold the ends over the roll.

Place the pastry-wrapped fillet on a baking tray with the folded ends down.

Brush the surface with beaten egg and decorate with lattice strips of leaves cut from pastry scraps.

Brush pastry again with beaten egg. Prick lightly with a fork and bake for 40 minutes or until the crust is a beautiful golden brown. Let it rest 15 minutes before slicing.

Serves 8

Pot Roast

This is a dish that tastes even better the next day. Mom would make this the night before and our side dishes were mashed potatoes, peas and carrots, and apple sauce. Sometimes she would make potato pancakes (see page 81)

> 4-5 lb. cross rib roast
> oil for browning meat
> 3 carrots, peeled and cut into large pieces
> 3 celery stalks, cut into large pieces
> 2 large onions, cut into large pieces
> 1 tbs. ground allspice
> 2 tbs. white vinegar
> Salt and pepper to taste
> Enough water to cover meat and vegetables
> 2 tbs. cornstarch mixed with 6 tbs. cold water
> Gravy Master seasoning and browning sauce

In a deep pot, heat oil to medium high and brown meat on all sides; add the vegetables and sauté, about 10 minutes.

Pour enough water in pot to cover roast half way up sides, add allspice, vinegar, salt and pepper and stir to blend; cover and cook over medium- high heat about 1 ½ hours, occasionally turning meat.

Remove meat, place on a platter and set aside. Remove your vegetables and strain in a sieve over your pot. Add your cornstarch and water mixture to the juices and stir until it thickens; add the gravy master to make gravy a deep dark brown.

Cut your meat against the grain into ½ inch slices and place back in pot and continue to cook another 30 minutes. Stirring often to prevent sticking on bottom.

Pulled Pork Roast

5-7 lb. Boston butt roast

Dry Rub

3 tbs. paprika
1 tbs. garlic powder
2 tbs. brown sugar
1 tbs. dry mustard
3 tbs. kosher salt
Your favorite barbeque sauce

I have found a Boston butt to be the best cut of meat for this recipe.

Mix the dry ingredients in a bowl and rub spice blend on all sides of the roast. Cover with plastic wrap and refrigerate overnight.

Preheat oven to 300 °

Place meat in a 9x13 roasting pan, bake covered with aluminum foil for the first 2 hours. Remove the foil and continue baking for another 4 hours. A thermometer stuck into the thickest part (not touching the bone) of the roast should read 170 °, but basically what you are looking for is the meat to fall off the bone when touched.

When the roast is done, remove from oven and allow it to rest for about 10 minutes.

While the pork is still warm, take two forks and starting at the top pull down on the roast. It will just fall off the bone (at this point your biggest challenge will be in not sneaking some of this delicious meat)

Lay pulled meat on a serving platter with your favorite sauce on the side.

In my house I always put leftovers to good use. With a little imagination, we can turn leftovers into a new dish. To make use of leftover pulled pork, prepare my baked beans (see pg. 84) and follow these instructions: First, shred the pork by hand and combine it with the beans. Next, bake the uncovered mixture at 350 degrees on the middle oven rack, for 30 minutes or until bubbly.

Serve with mashed potatoes and a tossed salad.

Another option is to smother pulled pork on a hero roll and layer with coleslaw, pickles, a slice of ham and Swiss cheese. Put your sandwich together and place on an ungreased- hot skillet, lightly cover the sandwich with aluminum foil and rest a heavy skillet on top of sandwich, pressing down if needed to flatten. When cheese starts to melt flip sandwich over for a few more minutes.
Serve with French fries or potato chips.

Sausage and Peppers

8 links of pork sausage, parboiled and cut into 1 inch circles
6 bell peppers, cleaned and cut into strips (you can used mixed colors)
2 large onion, sliced lengthwise
4 large potatoes, peeled and sliced
Oil for frying
Salt and pepper to taste

Preheat oven to 375°.

Boil sausage for 15 minutes to partially cook

Fry peppers and onions until tender, remove from pan and set aside.

Add oil to same frying pan and cook potatoes until almost done.

In a 9x13 baking dish, combine sausage, peppers and onions, potatoes, salt, pepper and blend. Bake 30 minutes or until bubbly, stirring occasionally.

Serves 4

Stuffed Cabbage

1 ½ lb. ground beef
1 cup uncooked rice
1 large onion sliced lengthwise
1 whole cabbage, core removed
1 8 oz. can sauerkraut
1 8 oz. can tomato sauce
Salt and pepper to taste
1 egg, beaten
Water to cover

Blanch the cabbage in boiling water, with a fork separate the leaves as they soften, placed removed leaves on a platter to cool until all leaves are cooked.

Cook rice for 22 minutes, drain.

In a bowl combine ground beef, beaten egg, cooked rice, salt and pepper.

Take a cooled Cabbage leaf, at stem end of leaf fill with ¼ cup of mixture. Roll once, tuck over both sides to center and roll to end of leaf. Set aside until all leaves are filled.

In a 3 quart pot over medium high heat, add onions, sauerkraut and any cabbage (chopped into chunks) that you didn't use for roll ups and sauté until onions are softened.

Place your filled rolls on top of onions. Add enough water to cover three-quarters of your rolls. Add the can of tomato sauce and give it all a swirl to blend.

Simmer over medium-low heat for 1 hour and 15 minutes, carefully stirring occasionally just to move it around.

Serves 2 rolls per person.

Roasted Turkey

Over the years, I have cooked turkey a variety of ways, including using different temperatures and brining. This recipe, however, was by far the best I have tried. The skin was crisp and the meat was very moist and tender.

    10–12 lb. turkey
    2 large onions, sliced
    4 oz. softened butter
    salt and pepper to taste
    2 cups water

Preheat oven to 325°.

Rinse turkey and pat dry inside and out. Place turkey, onions, and giblets in your roasting pan; rub the softened butter all over the turkey and season lightly with salt and pepper.

Add water and cover lightly with aluminum foil (remove this for the last hour of cooking to allow turkey to brown). Bake for 2 ½–3 ½ hours or until an instant-read meat thermometer registers 165° when inserted into the largest section of thigh (avoiding the bone). The turkey is so moist and tender cooked this way.

Gravy

Mix 3 tbs. cornstarch with 6 tbs. water and set aside.

Put juices and onions from turkey in a pot and bring to a rolling boil. Add the cornstarch mixture, stirring constantly as it thickens. Add salt and pepper to taste and Gravy Master for desired color.

Cooking Times for Turkey

8–12 lbs.	2 ½–3 ½ hours
12–16 lbs.	3 ½–4 ½ hours
16–20 lbs.	4–5 hours
20–24 lbs.	4 ½–6 hours

Shrimp Parmigiana

1 28-oz. can crushed tomatoes
1 medium onion, chopped
3 tbs. sugar
salt and pepper to taste
½ tsp. dried oregano
1 can of water, using empty tomato can
2 tbs. oil
1 lb. peeled and deveined raw shrimp
1 cup plain bread crumbs
3 tbs. grated Parmesan cheese
1 tsp. dried parsley flakes
1 egg, beaten
8 oz. shredded mozzarella cheese

Preheat oven to 350°.

Over medium-high heat, fry onions in oil until lightly golden. Add crushed tomatoes, sugar, water, oregano, salt, and pepper, and cook at low boil for 25 minutes.

In a bowl, combine bread crumbs, grated cheese, parsley flakes, salt, and pepper; in another bowl, add the beaten egg. Dip each shrimp in the egg batter and then the bread crumb mixture.

Fry shrimp in oil over medium-high heat to just put some color on the bread crumbs (about 1 minute on each side).

Put some sauce into an 8x13-inch baking dish, leaving enough sauce for top layer. Lay the shrimp on top of sauce. Sprinkle the mozzarella over the shrimp and cover with more sauce. Bake for 20 minutes.

Shrimp scampi butter (recipe below)
3 large cloves garlic
1 small shallot, chopped
2 tsp. fresh or dried parsley
1 tbs. lemon juice fresh or bottled
¼ lb. (one stick) butter, softened
¼ tsp. paprika
1 lb. peeled and deveined raw shrimp
1 lb. fettuccine
salt and pepper to taste

Shrimp Scampi Butter

In a food processor or by hand, finely chop garlic and shallots. Add parsley, lemon juice, and butter until thoroughly combined. Add salt, pepper, and paprika to taste. Use at once or can be frozen up to two months.

Melt ¼ cup garlic butter in a sauté pan over medium heat. Add shrimp and cook until shrimp are opaque in color.

When the fettuccine is cooked and drained, slide it onto a pretty platter. Pour your shrimp mixture on top along with the rest of the scampi butter and toss.

Serves 6 to 8

Sole with Crab Stuffing

1 tbs. vegetable oil
¼ cup chopped onion
¼ cup chopped green pepper
6 oz. can crab meat, cleaned and flaked
2 tbs. seasoned dry bread crumbs
½ tsp. dried parsley
½ tsp. salt (optional)
½ tsp. lemon pepper seasoning
2 sole fillets (½ lb. each), ½–¾ in. thick
½ cup tomato juice
¼ tsp. dried oregano
¼ tsp. dried basil
½ tsp. lemon juice
3 slices lemon, each cut in half

Preheat oven to 325°.

Grease baking pan and set aside.

Heat oil in small skillet. Add onion and green pepper, and sauté over medium heat until tender; remove from heat.

Stir in crab meat, bread crumbs, parsley, salt, and lemon pepper seasoning. Place one sole fillet on baking pan and spoon stuffing mixture onto it. Top with remaining fillet. Set aside.

In a small saucepan, combine tomato juice, oregano, basil and lemon juice and heat to a boil, reduce heat to medium and cook 1 minute. Pour half the sauce over the fillets and place the lemon slices on top.

Bake until fish flakes easily with fork, 50 to 60 minutes.

Serve with remaining sauce.

Makes 4 to 6 servings

Stuffed Peppers

6 peppers with flat bottoms
1 cup rice
1 ½ lbs. ground beef
1 beaten egg
¼ cup grated Romano cheese
3 tbs. plain bread crumbs
salt and pepper to taste
1 28-oz. can of tomato sauce

Preheat oven to 375°.

Cook the rice for 22 minutes and drain.

Cut off top of peppers remove seeds, rinse and pat dry.

In a bowl, add ground meat, rice, egg, grated cheese, bread crumbs, salt, and pepper; mix well, being careful not to break up your rice.

Coat the bottom of a baking pan with oil. Fill your peppers to top and place in pan; bake covered with foil wrap for 1 hour.

Remove foil and pour the tomato sauce over peppers. Sprinkle a little salt and pepper on top and cook another 30 minutes uncovered, occasionally spooning some of the sauce over the peppers. Peppers are done when you can easily insert a fork or knife at the base.

Veal Marsala

> 4 5-oz. veal cutlets
> ½ cup flour
> 2 tbs. butter
> 2 cups mushrooms, sliced
> 1 tbs. vegetable oil
> ½ cup marsala wine
> 1 tbs. fresh parsley chopped
> salt and pepper to taste

Lay veal between two pieces of waxed paper and flatten each cutlet with a mallet until about ⅛-inch thick. Dredge lightly in flour. Shake off any excess.

Melt butter in a skillet over medium heat. Add the mushrooms and cook until nicely browned, about 5 minutes. Remove mushrooms and set aside.

Add oil to the skillet and heat until very hot. Sauté veal quickly over high heat, about 1 minute on each side. Remove to a platter and keep warm.

Add marsala wine to skillet and simmer until it has reduced slightly, about 2 minutes. Add reserved mushrooms, salt, pepper, and chopped parsley; pour over warm veal.

Veal Parmigiana

2 28oz. cans crushed tomatoes
1 large onion, chopped
6 tbs. sugar
salt and pepper to taste
1 tsp. dried oregano
2 tbs. Oil for sauce
2 lbs. veal cutlets, sliced thin
2 cups plain bread crumbs
½ cup Romano cheese
1 tbs. fresh or dried parsley
1 lb. mozzarella, sliced thin, shredded or cubed
2 beaten eggs
Oil for frying cutlets

Preheat oven to 350 °

In a large pot, on medium high heat fry onions in the 2 tbs. oil until it just starts to get some color. Add crushed tomatoes, sugar, oregano, salt and pepper. Reduce heat and cook 30 minutes. (if sauce is too thick, just add a little water)

Combine bread crumbs, ¼ cup of grated cheese, parsley, salt and pepper in a bowl. In another bowl add your beaten eggs. Start by dipping a cutlet in the beaten eggs and then in the bread crumb mixture. Continue until all cutlets are breaded.

Add oil to a large frying pan, over medium high heat fry your cutlets to a light golden brown, about 2 minutes each side.

Spoon some sauce in a 9x13 baking dish, leaving some sauce for making layers. Place your veal cutlets in a single layer, top it with your mozzarella cheese, sprinkle some grated cheese and cover with sauce, continue to make your next layer following the same steps.

Bake uncovered for 45 minutes or until the cutlets are bubbly and tender.

Vegetables, Potatoes, and Side Dishes

Asparagus with Mozzarella
Chilled Sesame Asparagus
Broccoli with Garlic and Mozzarella
Creamed Cauliflower
Cauliflower with Mozzarella

Cheesy Potatoes
Potato Pancakes
Scalloped Potatoes with Cheese
Sweet Potatoes

Baked Beans
Bread Stuffing
Corn Casserole
Corn Fritters
Eggplant Parmigiana
Eggplant Rollatini
Rice Stuffing

When making a casserole, make an additional batch to freeze for another evening when you're short on time. Use within two months.

Boil all vegetables that grow above ground with a cover.

When cooking greens, add a teaspoon of sugar to the water to retain the fresh color.

To dress up buttered, cooked vegetables, sprinkle on some toasted sesame seeds, toasted chopped nuts, canned French fried onions, grated cheese, or slightly crushed croutons.

Asparagus with Mozzarella

1 bunch asparagus, trimmed and parboiled
8 oz. shredded mozzarella
2 oz. grated Romano cheese
2 tbs. butter
salt and pepper to taste

Preheat oven to 350°.

In a 8 × 8-inch baking dish, lay the asparagus evenly. Drop pats of butter here and there; sprinkle with mozzarella, grated cheese, salt, and pepper. Bake for 15–20 minutes or until cheese has melted.

Chilled Sesame Asparagus

2 lbs. fresh asparagus, trimmed
2 tbs. plus 2 tsp. dark sesame oil
1 tbs. plus 1 tsp. rice vinegar
1 tbs. plus 1 tsp. soy sauce
1 tsp. sugar
1 tbs. toasted sesame seeds

Cook asparagus in boiling water for 4–5 minutes; plunge asparagus into ice water to stop the cooking process. Drain, cover, and chill 2 hours.

Whisk together the sesame oil, vinegar, soy sauce, and sugar, and chill 2 hours.

Arrange asparagus on platter and spoon dressing evenly over top; sprinkle with toasted sesame seeds.

Broccoli with Garlic and Mozzarella

2 lbs. frozen broccoli florets, cooked and drained
1 tbs. garlic powder
½ lb. shredded mozzarella
3 tbs. grated Romano cheese
½ tsp. dried parsley
salt and pepper to taste
¼ cup plain bread crumbs
oil to drizzle

Preheat oven to 350°.

After you drain the cooked broccoli, put back in pot, add garlic powder, mozzarella, grated cheese, parsley, salt, and pepper, and stir until blended.

Spoon mixture into a greased 8 × 8-inch baking dish. Sprinkle the bread crumbs evenly on top and drizzle with a little oil. Bake uncovered for 20 minutes.

Creamed Cauliflower

1 pkg. frozen cauliflower florets, cooked and drained
2 tbs. butter
2 tbs. flour
2 cups milk
salt and white pepper to taste

In a deep pot make a roux by melting the butter and adding the flour, using the back of a spoon mash together making a smooth paste consistency being careful not to burn the flour and continue to cook for about another minute. Slowly add the milk stirring   until both cups of milk have been added. Add cauliflower, salt, pepper and cook another 20 minutes on low heat until desired thickness.

Cauliflower with Mozzarella

2 pkgs. frozen cauliflower, cooked, drained and mashed
8 oz. shredded mozzarella
¼ cup grated Romano cheese
Salt and pepper to taste

Preheat oven to 350 degrees

Mix all ingredients, spoon into a greased baking dish. Bake for 20 minutes or until cheese is melted and bubbly.

This was always a great way to get my kids to eat cauliflower.

Cheesy Potatoes

1 32-oz. bag of frozen hash brown or cubed potatoes
1 10 ¾ can cheddar cheese soup
8 oz. container of sour cream
12 oz. pkg. shredded cheddar cheese
1 cup milk

Preheat oven to 350°.

In a large bowl thoroughly mix all ingredients. Pour into a greased 9 × 11 inch baking dish; with a spoon, smooth the top evenly. Sprinkle with a little pepper and bake for 1 hour.

This is so delicious and creamy, you'll surely want seconds.

Serves 8

Potato Pancakes

2 ½ lbs. potatoes, coarsely shredded
1 grated large onion
⅓ cup flour
1 egg
1 tsp. salt
Oil for frying

Mix all ingredients together.

Heat oil in pan and drop in ¼-cup amounts of mixture. With spoon, spread to shape a pancake. Fry till golden brown; flip over and brown other side.

Place on a platter; keep warm while you cook the rest of the pancakes.

Serve with apple sauce and sour cream. Great as a side dish for pot roast (see page 61).

Scalloped Potatoes with Cheese

2 lbs. potatoes, cut into thin slices
2 tbs. butter, melted
½ tsp. salt
⅛ tsp. pepper
½ cup (2 oz.) shredded Gruyere cheese
1 cup hot milk

Preheat oven to 425°.

Coat an 11 × 7-inch baking dish with cooking spray and arrange half the potatoes in the dish. Drizzle with half the butter and sprinkle with half the salt, pepper, and cheese; repeat the next layer.

Pour hot milk over the potatoes and bake for 40 minutes or till tender.

Serves 7

Sweet Potatoes

 5 lbs. sweet potatoes or yams, boiled and peeled
 ¾ stick of butter
 1 ½ cups light brown sugar
 2 ½ cups maple syrup

Preheat oven to 375°.

In a large baking dish, make a single layer of potatoes sliced about ½ in thick, cut pats of butter over the potatoes (leaving enough for your next layer) sprinkle with brown sugar and continue your next layer until all potatoes are sliced.

Pour syrup over potatoes and bake for 1 ½ hours. Half way through cooking time I baste the potatoes with the syrup. These are always a big hit for Thanksgiving along with my stuffing (see pages 85 and 90).

Baked Beans

2 large cans pork and beans (we use Bush's original)
2 lbs. ground beef
1 large onion, chopped fine
1 large pepper, seeded and chopped fine
8 oz. of light brown sugar
11 oz. ketchup
Oil for frying

Preheat oven to 350°.

Brown meat, onion, and peppers in some oil and drain. Put back in pan and add sugar, ketchup and beans; heat until the sugar dissolves. Put in a 9 × 13-inch baking dish and bake for 30 minutes.

Bread Stuffing

    1 loaf sliced bread torn into small chunks
    1 stick of butter (8tbs.)
    2 medium onions, chopped fine
    3 stalks celery, chopped fine
    3 eggs
    1 ½ cup milk
    1 tbs. poultry seasoning
    salt and pepper to taste
    1 tbs. butter for top of stuffing before baking

The day before preparing this, I break my bread into a large bowl to let it get stale.

Preheat oven to 350°.

Melt butter in sauté pan. Add onions and celery and cook till tender with a light color; pour over the stale bread and mix well.

In another bowl beat your eggs and milk, and pour over bread; mix well to moisten the bread (if too dry, just add a little more milk).

Add salt, pepper, and poultry seasoning and mix well.

Add mixture to an 8 × 8-inch baking dish. Cut 1 tbs. butter in thin slices and stick into the stuffing. Bake for 45 minutes.

Corn Casserole

    2 15 ¼ oz. cans kernel corn drained
    2 15 ½ oz cans cream corn
    2 pkgs. corn muffin mix
    2 cups sour cream
    2 cups shredded cheddar cheese
    2 cups dried fried onions

Preheat oven to 350°.

In a bowl, mix all ingredients. Bake in a greased 13 × 9-inch baking dish for 1 hour and 15 minutes.

Your group will be asking for seconds on this one.

Corn Fritters

1 17 Oz. can of corn drained (reserve the liquid)
1 egg
2 ⅓ cups all-purpose baking mix (I use Bisquick)
Oil for frying

In the bowl containing the reserved corn liquid, add the egg, baking mix and blend until smooth, fold in the corn until well blended.

Add oil to a hot pan, carefully drop a full tablespoon of mixture into the pan and fry until golden brown, turn fritter over and brown on that side. Remove fritter and place on a paper towel to drain excess oil.

Serve hot, with warmed maple syrup on the side.

Eggplant Parmigiana

2 large eggplants, peeled and sliced in ½-in. circles
1 medium onion chopped fine
2 28-oz. cans crushed tomatoes
6 tbs. sugar
2 lbs. shredded mozzarella
½ cup grated Romano cheese
salt and pepper to taste
1 can water (Use tomato can; you may need to add a little more water if sauce is too thick.)
oil for frying

In a deep pot, lightly brown the onions; add the crushed tomatoes, sugar, salt, pepper, and water, and cook at a medium boil for 25 minutes.

Carefully add the eggplant slices into hot pan and fry until golden brown and almost cooked, about 3 minutes on each side. Place on paper towels to drain the excess oil.

My gang likes the eggplant just plain fried, but you can also dip your eggplant into beaten egg and bread crumbs before frying.

Preheat oven to 350°.

In a large baking dish, spoon some of the sauce to coat bottom, leaving some for all your layers. Place a layer of eggplant on top of the sauce; sprinkle with mozzarella and grated cheese, and spoon sauce on top of that. Begin again and continue layering until you run out of eggplant; finish with a layer of cheese and then sauce. Bake for 45 minutes.

Eggplant Rollatini

2 large eggplants, peeled and sliced lengthwise into ½ in. slices
1 medium onion, chopped
2 28 oz. cans crushed tomatoes
6 tbs. sugar
6 cloves garlic, chopped fine
1 3-lb. container ricotta with 2 beaten eggs added
1 lb. pkg. mozzarella, shredded
½ cup grated Romano cheese
oil
1 can of water (use tomato can)

In a deep pot, add oil and fry onions until a light golden; add garlic and stir a few seconds. Add crushed tomatoes, sugar, salt, pepper, and water, and cook at a medium boil for 25 minutes.

Carefully add the eggplant slices into hot pan and fry until golden and almost cooked, about 3 minutes on each side, and place on paper towels to drain the excess oil.

Preheat oven to 350°.

Add the shredded mozzarella and grated cheese to the ricotta and beaten egg mixture, and mix well.

In a large baking dish, ladle some of your sauce (save some for your top layer) and proceed to fill with your slices.

Lay a slice of eggplant flat and spoon the ricotta mixture on top. Roll up and place seam side down in baking dish; ladle more sauce over, covering completely. Bake for 30 minutes or until bubbly.

Rice Stuffing

    1 lb. box rice
    2 eggs, beaten
    1 oz. chicken or turkey liver
    ½ cup grated Romano cheese
    ¾ tbs. dried parsley
    salt and pepper to taste
    butter

Preheat oven to 350°.

Boil rice 22 minutes and drain. Put in a large bowl and add the beaten eggs; mix well with a fork.

While rice is cooking, melt 2 tbs. butter and fry the liver; cut into small pieces.

Add liver, grated cheese, parsley, salt, and pepper to cooked rice and mix well; spoon mixture into a greased 9 × 13-inch baking dish and bake for 45 minutes

I always had to make both of my stuffing recipes for the holidays to make everyone happy.

Sauces and Pasta Dishes

Calamari Sauce
Crab Sauce
Frying Pan Sauce
Meat Sauce
Sunday Sauce

Baked Lasagna
Fettuccine Alfredo
Linguine with Garlic Sauce
Manicotti
Pasta Primavera
Penne with Bleu Cheese

Cook pasta al dente (slightly chewy to the bite).

To prevent pasta from boiling over, place a wooden spoon across top of pot as you are cooking.

Calamari Sauce

2 lbs. calamari, cleaned, drained, and sliced in circles
6 oz. can tomato paste
1 small can tomato sauce
1 medium onion, sliced thin
2 tbs. olive oil
1 tsp. dried basil
salt and pepper to taste
water as needed

Cook onions in oil until limp and clear. Add the paste along with a
½ can of water (using the paste can) and stir.

Add the tomato sauce, basil, salt, pepper, and calamari. Cook
uncovered for 45 minutes to 1 hour at a little more than a simmer,
stirring frequently. If it gets too thick, just add a little water.

This tastes better if made earlier in the day or the day before.

Make the pasta of your choice and drain. Put back in pot and add
some of the sauce to coat. Slide pasta onto a platter. Ladle the rest of
the calamari sauce over it and serve.

Crab Sauce

2 large cans tomato puree
1 6 oz. can tomato paste
1 large onion chopped fine
4 cloves of garlic, chopped fine
6 tbs. sugar
1 tsp. crushed red pepper flakes (You can leave this out or add more if you like hot.)
oil
salt and pepper to taste
water
2 doz. Blue claw crabs, cooked in boiling water until shell turns red

Crabs should be purchased only if active and to be cooked the same day of purchase.

When crabs are cool enough to handle, break off the claws and remove the top shell. Rinse under water to remove the stringy gills found under both sides of the shell. Using a vegetable brush, scrub away any dirt left on the remaining shell.

In a large, deep pot, cook the onions in the oil; when onions are a golden color, add the garlic. Add the tomato puree and paste. Fill the 3 empty tomato cans with water and add to pot along with the sugar, hot pepper flakes, salt, and pepper; stir until blended. Add the crabs and cook on a low boil for 1 ½ hours.

Cook your favorite pasta and drain. Put back in pot and add some sauce to coat. Pour onto a big serving platter and surround with crabs. Ladle more sauce on top and serve.

Frying Pan Sauce (Marinara)

1 large can crushed tomatoes
2 cloves garlic, chopped fine
1 small onion, chopped into small pieces
2 tbs. fresh chopped basil
3 tbs. sugar
2 tbs. oil
salt and pepper to taste
½ can of water
fresh basil for presentation

Using a large frying pan, fry the onion in the oil until golden. Add the garlic and toss around a few seconds. Add tomatoes, water, sugar, basil, salt, and pepper, and cook for 30 minutes at a medium boil.

Cook your favorite pasta. Drain and add it right into the frying pan and toss. Slide it onto a pretty platter and place some fresh basil in center of platter.

Meat Sauce

2 28-oz. cans tomato puree
1 6-oz. can tomato paste
2 lbs. ground beef, browned and drained
1 medium onion, chopped
3 cloves garlic, chopped fine
6 tbs. sugar
oil
salt and pepper to taste
water from the tomato cans

Brown your meat and then set aside in a strainer to drain the grease.

In a large pot, brown the onions in the 3 tbs. oil; add garlic and toss a few minutes, being careful not to burn garlic. Add tomato puree, paste, water from the 3 cans, salt, and pepper; stir well and add the cooked ground beef. Cook for 1 hour and 15 minutes.

Sunday Sauce

Sunday was a big day in my house when I was growing up, probably because we always had company. Mommy would always make this sauce. She was the kind of mother who, if she knew someone liked a dish, it was there when they visited. I try to follow in her footsteps now …

    2 28-oz. cans tomato puree
    1 6-oz. can tomato paste
    1 large onion, chopped
    3 cloves garlic, chopped fine
    6 tbs. sugar
    5 or 6 leaves fresh basil, coarsely chopped
    salt and pepper to taste
    water from the cans
    oil

In a large deep pot, heat oil and fry onions to a golden brown; add garlic and stir quickly. Add tomato puree, tomato paste, water, sugar, salt, pepper and basil. Stir to combine with total cooking time 2 hours on medium-low.

Now we'll start with the meats. We'll prepare each one individually so as not to get all our ingredients mixed up. As you fry your meats, just keep adding them to your sauce pot.

The sausage is the easiest. In a large frying pan, fry 6 links of sweet or hot sausage in a little oil to brown on all sides, and add to sauce pot.

Meatballs

    2 lbs. ground beef
    3 beaten eggs
    ¼ cup grated Romano cheese
    2 cloves garlic, chopped fine
    ¼ cup plain bread crumbs

1 tbs. parsley
salt and pepper to taste

In a bowl, mix all the ingredients well. If it's too loose, just add more bread crumbs. Make the meatballs the size equivalent to a ½-cup measure. Fry in oil on both sides to a light brown and place in sauce pot.

Beef Braciole

This is an Italian specialty, best made from thin slices of beef rump, top round, or bottom round. The slices are individually stuffed with a filling, rolled, and tied.

2 4-5 oz. slices of beef, pounded to ¼ in. thickness (Take care not to tear the meat.)
1 hard-boiled egg, cut in half and then each half sliced into three pieces
1 cup plain bread crumbs
3 tbs. grated Romano cheese
1 tsp. dried parsley
salt and pepper to taste
1 beaten egg

In a bowl, mix bread crumbs, cheese, parsley, salt, pepper, and egg, and stir to make a thick mixture.

Lay the meat slices flat and spread half of the stuffing on each slice, leaving a border on each end. Put 3 pieces of the hard-boiled egg on each slice; roll up, tucking in the sides to form a tight, neat packet. Tie securely with kitchen twine or toothpicks

Fry on all sides in oil and add to sauce pot.

When sauce is cooked, take the braciole out and remove the strings. Cut into 1-inch slices and place on a platter with the rest of your meat.

Baked Lasagna

I use the meat sauce recipe (see page 96) for my lasagna. This way I know I'll have enough sauce to put this dish together.

Preheat oven to 375°.

> meat sauce
> 1 lb. lasagna
> 1 2-lb. container of ricotta mixed with 1 beaten egg
> ½ cup grated Romano cheese
> 1 lb. mozzarella, shredded or cubed

Add your lasagna to boiling water (I put some oil in boiling water to keep macaroni from sticking) and cook about 10–12 minutes. Drain and separate the noodles.

In a 13 × 9 × 3 inch baking pan, add some sauce to cover bottom. Start layering noodles, overlapping the ends a little to hold the sauce. Spread ⅓ of the ricotta over noodles and ¼ of the mozzarella; sprinkle 1 tbs. grated cheese on top and cover with sauce. Continue with next layer until all noodles are used, with the final layer being sauce. You will have four layers of pasta and three layers of filling..

Bake for 1 hour and let sit 15 minutes (for easier cutting) before serving.

Serves 8 to 10

Baked ziti is made this way also; just change your pasta to make it an easier dish to put together.

Fettuccine Alfredo

1 lb. fresh fettuccine if available; if not, dried will work fine
1 stick butter
1 cup heavy cream
1 cup grated Parmigiano-Reggiano cheese saving some to
sprinkle on top
salt and pepper to taste

Bring 6 quarts water to full boil and add fettuccine; cook 6–8 minutes, until tender but firm al dente. Drain.

Melt butter in large skillet. Add fettuccine, heavy cream, cheese, salt, and pepper, and toss over low heat until fettuccine is well coated. Sprinkle the extra cheese and serve immediately.

Linguine with Garlic Sauce

1 lb. linguine
⅓ cup extra-virgin olive oil
3 large cloves garlic, chopped fine
¼ tsp. crushed red pepper (can be omitted)
¼ cup finely chopped fresh parsley
1 ½ tbs. butter
1 tsp. finely grated lemon zest

Cook linguine in large pot of salted boiling water 6–8 minutes; save
¾ cup of pasta water and drain the rest.

Meanwhile, gently heat olive oil, garlic, red pepper, and parsley in
a covered pan over very low heat just until garlic is soft (be careful
not to burn garlic).

In a large serving bowl, add the pasta, garlic mixture, ¾ cup pasta
water, and rest of ingredients, and toss well.

Serves 6

meat sauce (see page 96)
1 cup flour
1 cup water
2 eggs
3 lbs. ricotta mixed with 2 beaten eggs
8 oz. mozzarella, shredded or small cubes
1 cup grated Romano cheese
1 ½ tbs. dried parsley
salt

Preheat oven 350°.

Crepes

In a bowl mix the flour, a pinch of salt, water, and 2 eggs with a blender or a hand mixer until smooth and feathery; refrigerate for 30 minutes to allow the flour to absorb the liquid and give the gluten in the flour a chance to relax.

Heat a nonstick crepe pan and coat with some cooking spray; pour 2 tbs. batter in heated pan and rotate in a circle motion to coat the pan to edges. When the edges start to curl up, turn over with a fork, spatula, or fingers (I find my fingers work best); cook on other side for a minute.

Place cooked crepe on a platter and cover with a paper towel; continue making the rest of batter.

Filling

In a large bowl stir the ricotta with the 2 beaten eggs, grated cheese, mozzarella, and parsley and mix well.

Have a baking dish ready with a layer of meat sauce on bottom.

Lay a crepe flat; put some mixture in center and fold, gently press on it to spread the ricotta evenly to almost the ends of the folded crepe. Lay crepes seam side down in baking dish. Ladle more sauce to cover all the crepes and bake for at least 40 minutes.

1 large zucchini, cut into thinly-sliced circles
2 medium carrots, peeled, cut into thin circles
¾ cup fresh or frozen peas
1 medium broccoli, chopped
salt
½ cup grated Romano cheese
¼ cup plus 1 tbs. olive oil
2 peeled and thinly sliced garlic cloves
1 lb. fettuccine, penne, spaghetti, or desired pasta

Bring water to a boil in a 2-quart pot and add the zucchini, carrots, fresh or frozen peas, and broccoli. Do not cover pot. Boil for 5 minutes; drain and set aside.

Cook pasta according to package directions, adding salt and 1 tbs. olive oil to prevent sticking. Just before the pasta is done to your liking, add ¼ cup olive oil and the sliced garlic to a sauce pan, and heat over medium heat until the garlic starts to brown, about 2 minutes.

Drain the pasta and save 1 cup of the liquid. Add all the vegetables to the pasta pot along with the reserved water and the oil and garlic, and mix well. Serve hot, sprinkled with grated cheese.

Penne with Bleu Cheese

1 lb. penne pasta
½ lb. good, smooth bleu cheese plus some extra to crumble on
top before serving
4 tbs. butter
2 pints heavy cream
2 beaten egg yolks
Salt and pepper to taste
¼ cup grated Romano cheese

In a pot, melt butter and add ½ lb. bleu cheese. Add salt, pepper, heavy cream and bring to a boil. Add egg yolks and stir vigorously.

Cook and drain your penne and place on a pretty serving platter. Pour bleu cheese mixture over your pasta and toss, sprinkle with grated cheese and crumbled pieces of bleu cheese and serve immediately.

Serves 4 as a main dish or 6 as a first course.

Cakes

Baking is a science of ingredients, and because of this, it is known to be more difficult than cooking. A good cook can create a dish to their taste, but baking is about exact measurements and timing, with the rewards profound and appreciated, here is a collection of my family and friends favorites.

Carrot Cake
Cream Cheese Biscuit Cake
Crumb Cake
Flag Cake
German Chocolate Cake
Ladyfinger Chocolate Mousse Cake
Pound Cake
Tiramisu

Fill cakes two-thirds full and spread into corners or sides, leaving a slight hollow in center.

Cake is done when it shrinks from the center of the pan or springs back when you touch lightly with your finger.

After removing cake from oven, place on a rack for 5 minutes. This allows the sides of cake to loosen and then you can turn it out on a rack to finish cooling.

Do not frost cakes until completely cooled.

Carrot Cake

  2 cups sugar
  1 ½ cups vegetable oil
  4 eggs
  2 ¼ cups sifted flour
  2 tsp. salt
  2 tsp. baking soda
  2 tsp. cinnamon
  3 cups grated carrots

Preheat oven to 300°.

Combine sugar, oil, and eggs. Beat 2 minutes and add the flour, salt, baking soda, and cinnamon. Fold in carrots.

Grease and flour a 9 × 13-inch baking pan. Pour batter into pan and bake for 1 hour and 15 minutes. Let cool completely,

Invert pan on a cake dish and make frosting.

Cream Cheese Frosting

  8 oz. cream cheese, softened
  2 sticks butter
  1 box confectioners' sugar
  ½ tsp. vanilla extract

Mix all ingredients together until smooth and creamy. With a serrated knife, slice the cake so that you can remove the top. Spread evenly with a layer of frosting; replace the cover and finish frosting top and sides.

Cream Cheese Biscuit Cake

⅓ cup walnuts, chopped
½ cup sugar
1 tsp. cinnamon
2 pkgs. biscuit rolls
3 tbs. melted butter
1 8oz. pkg. cream cheese, cut into 20 chunks or slices

Preheat oven to 375°.

In a bowl mix the nuts, sugar, and cinnamon, and set aside.

Melt butter and pour in a Bundt pan; roll it around until all surfaces are covered. Sprinkle 1 tbs. of the nut mixture on bottom and sides of pan.

Flatten a biscuit and top with a chunk of cream cheese and a tsp. of nut mixture; roll up.

Start laying the biscuits in Bundt pan in a circle. Biscuits should overlap each other for the first 10. Do the next layer going in the opposite direction. With my hands, I press it down a little so they all stick to each other.

Bake approximately 20 minutes and invert on platter and cool before cutting.

Crumb Cake

　　1 box yellow cake mix
　　1 lb. margarine melted
　　4 cups flour
　　1 cup sugar
　　3 tsp. cinnamon
　　1 tsp. vanilla extract

Preheat oven to 350°.

Grease and flour a jelly roll pan. Prepare cake mix as directed on box. Bake 20 minutes until firm but not brown. While cake is baking, make your crumb topping.

Put dry ingredients in a bowl and pour melted margarine over top. Mix with a spoon until lumpy. I also use my hands on this one to really blend it. Sprinkle topping over cake; put back in oven and bake another 15 minutes.

Cut into squares and sprinkle with confectioners' sugar when cool.

Flag Cake

2 18-oz. boxes of chocolate or yellow cake mix, prepared and baked according to package directions
1 16 oz. can of vanilla frosting
3 cups heavy cream
⅓ cup confectioners' sugar
2 tsp. vanilla extract
2 pints small strawberries
1 ½ cups blueberries
mini marshmallows

Bake cakes in two 15 × 10-inch jelly roll pans lined with waxed paper. Cool and turn cakes out of pans.

Spread 1 can, 16 oz., of ready-to-spread vanilla frosting between the two cake layers and stack them together.

To make the cake look like it is waving, start by cutting both ends straight down. On the top, start on the left and gradually go to the right, going into the cake slightly near the center. Then go back up and continue to other side. On the bottom, from the left start to make a small half moon coming to edge and continue to make another half moon finishing on the right of the cake.

Whip 3 cups heavy cream until stiff peaks form, adding ⅓ cup confectioners' sugar and two tsp. vanilla extract. Spread whipped cream on top and sides of cake.

Slice two pints small strawberries; arrange slices of strawberries on cake to make the seven stripes.

Place a field of blueberries in upper left-hand corner.

Cut mini marshmallows into four pieces and place on blueberries to represent the fifty states.

This cake made a big hit when we brought it to a 4th of July block party.

German Chocolate Cake

    4 oz. sweet chocolate melted
    ½ cup boiling water
    1 cup butter or margarine
    2 cups sugar
    4 eggs, separated
    1 tsp. vanilla extract
    2 cups flour
    1 tsp. baking soda
    ½ tsp. salt
    1 cup buttermilk
    Coconut pecan filling and frosting (recipe below)

Preheat oven to 350°.

Melt chocolate and cool.

Cream butter and sugar. Beat in egg yolks; stir in vanilla extract and chocolate.

Mix flour, soda, and salt. Beat flour mixture into butter and sugar mixture, alternating with buttermilk.

Beat egg whites until stiff peaks form; fold into batter. Pour batter into three 9-inch layer pans, lined on bottoms with waxed paper.

Bake for 30 minutes or until cake springs back when lightly pressed in center. Cool 15 minutes; remove and cool on rack.

Coconut Pecan Filling and Frosting

    14 oz. can of condensed milk
    ½ cup water
    3 egg yolks
    1 tsp. vanilla extract
    1 stick butter

1 ⅓ cups pecans, chopped (Reserve 10 whole pecan halves for garnish.)
1 ¾ cups flaked coconut

Cook the milk, eggs, and water over a double boiler until thickened. Then add the vanilla extract and butter, and whisk in until it is melted and smooth. Add the chopped pecans and coconut.

Chocolate Frosting (optional)

1 stick butter
9 Bakers German chocolate squares, melted and cooled
1 ½ cups powdered sugar
1 tsp. vanilla extract
1 ½ tbs. milk

Mix butter and chocolate in mixing bowl. Stir in powdered sugar; beat vanilla extract and milk until smooth and of spreading consistency.

Assembly

Divide the filling evenly between the three cakes. Put the first layer down and then spread the filling over it evenly; repeat with the next two layers covering the top.

Cover sides of the cake with chocolate frosting.

For garnish, you can place pecan halves around the top edge. You can also add a maraschino cherry half next to the pecan half.

Note: You can shave off any high spots with a bread knife to make the cakes flatter so they will stack evenly. You can also use any scraps from the shavings to fill in any low spots.

Ladyfinger Chocolate Mousse Cake

4 squares unsweetened chocolate
¾ cups sugar
⅓ cup milk
6 eggs, separated
1 ½ cups unsalted butter
1 ½ cups confectioners sugar
⅛ tsp. salt
1 ½ tsp. vanilla extract
3 dozen ladyfingers split
¾ cups heavy cream, whipped
chopped pistachios and shaved unsweetened chocolate for decorating top.

Melt chocolate in double boiler.

Combine granulated sugar, milk, and egg yolks in separate bowl and beat; mix into chocolate and cook until smooth and thick. Set aside to cool.

Cream butter well and add ¾ cup confectioners' sugar; cream thoroughly. Add to chocolate and mix well.

Beat egg whites and salt until stiff. Gradually beat in ¾ cup confectioners' sugar; fold into chocolate mixture. Add vanilla extract and set aside.

Line a deep 9-inch spring form pan with ladyfingers on bottom and standing up on sides. Pour a layer of chocolate mixture over and cover with more ladyfingers. Continue making layers, ending with the chocolate mixture.

Chill overnight. The next day release sides of pan and remove; place on a serving dish and spread the whipped heavy cream on before serving. For a pretty presentation, tie a ribbon around sides and serve.

Pound Cake

This is a pound cake that will fast become a family favorite. It makes a nice big cake and can be served many ways. My family's favorite way is toasted and buttered.

1 lb. butter
3 cups sugar
9 eggs
1 cup milk
4 cups flour
2 heaping tsp. baking powder
2 tsp. vanilla extract

Preheat oven to 375°.

In a bowl, put eggs, milk, and vanilla extract, and set aside.

In another bowl combine flour and baking powder and set aside

In a large bowl, cream butter and sugar until smooth; alternately add some of the liquid mixture and then the dry mixture, blending after each addition, until all ingredients are incorporated and blended well.

Pour mixture into a greased and floured angel food pan. Tap pan on table to get air bubbles out. Bake for 1 hour to 1 hour and 15 minutes or until a toothpick inserted in center comes out dry.

Tiramisu

6 egg yolks
¾ cup white sugar
⅔ cup milk
1 ¼ cups heavy cream
½ tsp. vanilla extract
1 lb. mascarpone cheese
¼ cup strong brewed coffee, room temperature
2 tbs. rum
2 3-oz. pkgs ladyfinger cookies
1 tbs. unsweetened cocoa powder

In a medium saucepan, whisk together egg yolks and sugar until well blended. Whisk in milk and cook over medium heat, stirring constantly, until mixture boils. Boil gently for 1 minute, remove from heat and allow to cool slightly. Cover tightly and chill in refrigerator 1 hour.

Whisk the mascarpone cheese into the yolk mixture until a smooth consistency.

In a medium bowl, beat cream with vanilla extract until stiff peaks form.

In a small bowl, combine coffee and rum. Split ladyfingers in half lengthwise and drizzle with coffee mixture.

Arrange half of soaked ladyfingers in bottom of a 7 × 11-inch dish. Spread half of mascarpone mixture over ladyfingers, and then half of whipped cream over that. Repeat layers and sprinkle with cocoa. Cover and refrigerate 4–6 hours, until set.

I use a little less rum and I don't make the coffee too strong. Use the best mascarpone cheese you can find.

Cookies

Ball Cookies
Butter Cookies
Chocolate Chip Cookies
Christmas Bow Tie Cookies
Date Ball Cookies
Fig Cookies
Krumkake Cookies
Pignoli Cookies
Pizzelle Cookies
Rainbow Cookies
Rugelach
Sugar Cookies

If you only have one cookie sheet on hand, line it with parchment paper; while one batch is baking, load a second sheet of parchment paper to have another batch ready to bake. Just slide first batch off and slide the cookie sheet under the second batch, which also makes for easier cleaning.

Bake one cookie sheet at a time, using the middle rack.

Ball Cookies

1 stick plus 3 tbs. butter, softened
1 cup sugar
6 eggs
4 cups flour
6 tsp. baking powder
1 tsp. vanilla extract

Preheat oven to 350°.

Mix all ingredients well. Take full tablespoon amounts of dough and roll into balls. Place on ungreased cookie sheet half an inch apart and bake for 10–15 minutes or until light golden on bottom (top will be white). Place on a rack to cool.

Icing

1 cup confectioners' sugar
¼ tsp. vanilla extract
3–4 tbs. milk

In bowl, mix ingredients until smooth dip tops of cookies into icing and set on rack to dry.

Butter Cookies

2 ¼ cups flour
¾ cup sugar
¼ tsp. baking powder
1 cup softened butter
2 eggs
1 tsp. vanilla extract

Preheat oven to 375°.

In a large bowl, put your butter and sugar, and with two knives, cut to make a coarse and crumbly mixture; add eggs and vanilla extract and mix well.

Add flour and baking powder and mix until all blended; this is a thick batter, so I find it better to use my hands for this step.

Fill tube of cookie press and make desired shapes onto a cookie sheet and bake for 12 minutes or until edges have golden color.

I always have to make two batches of these because the kids eat them as they come out of oven.

Chocolate Chip Cookies

½ cup butter, softened
1 cup packed light brown sugar
¾ cup granulated sugar
2 large eggs
1 ½ tsp. vanilla extract
¼ cup sour cream
2 ½ cups flour
1 tsp. baking powder
½ tsp. baking soda
½ tsp. salt
1 11.5 pkg. of chocolate chips or chunks
1 cup pecans, chopped

Preheat oven to 375 degrees

In a large bowl, beat butter and sugar on low until light and fluffy. Add eggs, vanilla extract, sour cream and beat on medium high for 2 minutes.

Stir in dry ingredients and add chocolate chips and pecans.

On an un-greased cookie sheet, place about ¼ cup of mixture and bake for 14-16 minutes.

These are great big delicious cookies and you can also make ice cream sandwiches with them.

Christmas Bow Tie Cookies

1 stick (8tbs.) butter melted
2 tbs. baking powder
1 tsp. vanilla extract
6 eggs
½ cup sugar
4 cups of flour and more as needed
½ gallon oil
pizza cutter
dishes for cookies before frying
brown bag, cut open to cool cookies on counter

In a large bowl with a mixer or hand beater, beat the 6 eggs and sugar, add the melted butter, vanilla extract, and baking powder and beat until well blended.

Now start adding flour and keep adding a cup at a time until it all comes together, then turn the dough out onto table and start kneading the dough. Keep adding flour and kneading until the dough is shiny and elastic. Shape into a log, cover with plastic wrap and set aside.

Preheat your fryer or deep pot of oil to 375°.

On a floured surface, make a slice of dough about 2 inches wide and roll out to a thin sheet (don't worry about the shape).

With pizza cutter make 2-in.strips. If the strips are very long, cut them in half.

In the center of each strip, cut a slit. Take one end of cookie and put it through the slit; give it a little tug, and place on a floured dish (this helps them not to stick to each other while you make all the cookies). You can make two layers on each dish, but sprinkle a little more flour before starting a second layer. Make all your cookies before you start frying them.

If using a deep fryer, place 3 cookies in the basket (when I use a large wide-top pot, I fry 6 cookies at a time). The cookies will float right to the top. (If they don't, your oil is not hot enough; just lift them up and wait until it's the right temperature, even if you have to raise the temperature a little.)

When the cookies start showing color on edges, with a fork flip them over to cook on other side. With a slotted spoon, lift cookies and place on brown bag to cool. After you make a few batches, move the cooled cookies to large pan to make room for more hot cookies.

For presentation, put them on a holiday platter and sprinkle with confectioners' sugar. You can also pour some honey on them instead of the sugar.

These cookies are absolutely fantastic.

Date Ball Cookies

    1 pkg. chopped dates
    1 ½ cups sugar
    2 sticks of butter (1/2 lb.)
    2 tsp. vanilla extract
    2 eggs
    1 pkg. coconut flakes
    ½ cup chopped walnuts
    3-4 cups rice krispie cereal

In a bowl, beat eggs and sugar; stir in chopped dates.

In a medium pot, melt butter and add the egg and date mixture; simmer over low heat while stirring constantly for 10 minutes.

Remove from stove, add vanilla extract, rice cereal and nuts; make teaspoon size balls, roll into the coconut flakes and place on a tray to set.

Fig Cookies

Growing up in my Italian family, there were two big traditions. One was celebrating the feast of Saint Joseph and the other was making the fig cookies.

These cookies were a big part of our holiday and I remember my mom, aunts, and grandparents all in the kitchen working together and laughing. What a system they had going! Grandma, Mommy, Aunt Sophie, and Aunt Katie would sit on chairs in the center of the kitchen facing each other, and Grandpa had this big wooden tabletop that he placed on their laps. Then Daddy and Uncle Tony would put all the prepared ingredients on the tabletop, and they would start making these beautifully designed cookies. Once the cookies started to come out of the oven (under the watchful eye of Grandpa), someone else was there ready to frost and sprinkle them. Then they would lay a sheet on one of the beds and place the cookies there to dry and that's where they would find me, my sister, brother and cousins.

What cherished memories I have from this event, in a time when it was all about family. It's time to share this recipe with you. My hopes are that I can bring this to your table and the memories can go on. When you make this cookie, please e-mail me and let me know if this was the best fig cookie you have ever had.

OK, let's get cooking.

Now we made a triple batch of this recipe because my grandparents would give so many to friends, but you can even cut this recipe in half, as I have done many times.

    7 lbs. flour
    3 lbs. melted and cooled vegetable shortening
    1 lb. sugar, melted in 2 cups hot water
    5 lbs. dried figs with ends removed
    2 ½ lbs. roasted filberts, skinned

1 large jar dried mixed fruit
2 tsp. cinnamon
½ lb. milk chocolate (chopped in small pieces)
box of confectioners' sugar
milk
small rolling pin (in those days, we sawed a wooden broom to make a 10-inch rolling pin)
Nonpareils for decorating

Filling

After you have snipped the hard top of the figs, boil them in water until very tender; drain but save the water.

In a 375° preheated oven, roast your filberts. (When cooled, rub them together and the skins fall off. Not all will come off, but as long as most does, it's OK.)

In a food processor, grind all your figs (will have to do a few batches) until they look like a paste; place in a large bowl. Next grind your filberts, mixed fruit, and chocolate; add to fig bowl along with the cinnamon and really mix well (many times I get right in there and use my hands).

Now is the time to put about 1 cup of the fig water into mixture and mix well. This gives it so much extra flavor.

Cookie Dough

I always put a vinyl table cloth on the kitchen table and pour all my flour onto it. Make a center well and add cooled shortening and melted sugar; start bringing the flour into the center and start working it together until all has been combined. Then start kneading until a nice, smooth texture is achieved.

Preheat oven to 375°.

To make the cookie, cut a piece of dough and roll thin. Put a nice spoonful of fig mixture in center and fold over sides to cover filling.

Roll the cookie a little and lay it seam side down and squeeze the ends closed; then press on the cookie gently to make it all flatter and even. With a knife, make a slit on the center of cookie and open it, then on both sides make little cuts into the cookie and open those as well. I have a picture of this cookie on the website for you to get a better understanding of what it looks like.

Place on an ungreased cookie sheet and bake for 35–40 minutes or until they've turned a golden color on bottom. (The top won't have that color, so turn the broiler on in oven to color top of cookie, but stand there watching because it browns fast!) As soon as you take the cookies out of oven, place on a cooling rack and brush the frosting on the cookies immediately while still hot and sprinkle with nonpareils.

Make your frosting while the cookies are baking. Mix the confectioners' sugar with milk to a smooth, loose (but not watery) texture.

Enjoy!

Krumkake Cookies

These deliciously light cookies are baked on a pizzelle machine.

> 4 eggs
> 1 cup sugar
> ½ cup melted butter
> 5 tbs. whipping cream
> 1 tsp. vanilla extract
> ¾ cup flour
> 2 tsp. cornstarch

Heat your pizzelle iron until ready light goes on. (When a few sprinkles of water skitter around on the surface, iron is ready.)

Beat all ingredients until smooth; drop 1 tsp. batter on each side of iron and close gently. I count to 15 and gently lift cover; these will be a delicate light color. With a knife, gently lift one cookie and very quickly roll it into a cigar shape and place on a cookie sheet to cool. Get the next cookie immediately.

When I have a bunch of cookies on sheet, I just move them to a pan until I'm ready to serve them. Continue until batter is finished; this will make about 6 dozen cookies.

For presentation, place on a holiday platter and sprinkle with confectioners' sugar.

These cookies are so light and delicate and I bet you can't just eat one.

Pignoli Cookies

1 lb. almond paste (Your local bakery will sell this and for much less than the supermarket.)
1 ⅓ cup sugar
1 tbs. honey
⅛ tsp. cinnamon
¼ tsp. lemon juice
½ tsp. vanilla extract
4 egg whites
6 oz. bag of pignoli nuts, poured into a small bowl
confectioners' sugar

This cookie goes into the freezer as soon as you take it out of the oven, so make sure there is a flat surface to lay the cookie tray on. (Lay a towel on frozen foods before placing hot cookie tray on it.)

Preheat oven to 325°.

In a large bowl, mix paste and sugar until well blended. (I use my hands first to break up the paste to a crumbly texture.) Mix in honey, cinnamon, lemon juice, and vanilla extract; beat in egg whites (beat well after each addition). Mixture will be sticky.

Line your cookie sheet with parchment paper. Place a full tablespoon of mixture in bowl with nuts to coat top; carefully lift and place on cookie sheet with nuts facing up.

Sprinkle with confectioners' sugar and bake 25 minutes. Immediately place in your freezer for 2 hours.

After 2 hours you can easily take them off cookie sheet and place in a tightly covered container until you are ready to serve.

These cookies are better than what you can get in any bakery. Try them and let me know what you think.

Pizzelle Cookies

6 eggs
1 cup sugar
1 cup oil
1 bottle anise extract (1 oz.)
3 ½ cups flour
4 tsp. baking powder
pizzelle machine

Heat your pizzelle machine (when light goes on, it's ready). Beat eggs and sugar until well blended; add oil, anise extract, and baking powder, and mix; add flour in two additions and beat to a smooth, thick texture.

Place a teaspoon of mixture on each side of machine and slowly close cover; count to 15 and gently open cover. Cookie should be a light golden color. With a knife, lift cookie out and place on wax paper to cool.

Serve on tray and sprinkle with confectioners' sugar.

Rainbow Cookies

4 eggs, separated
1 cup sugar
½ lb. butter, softened
2 cups flour
8 oz. almond filling
6 oz. chocolate chips
1 small jar raspberry preserves (seedless)
1 small jar apricot jam
yellow, red, and green food coloring
three 12 ⅛ × 8 ¼ × 1 3/16-inch pans (greased and lined with waxed paper that has also been greased)

Preheat oven to 350°.

Beat egg whites to stiff texture and set aside.

In a large bowl, cream the sugar, egg yolks, almond filling, and butter; slowly add flour; fold egg whites into mixture.

Put 1 ½ cup of mixture in each of three smaller bowls and color one yellow, one red, and one green.

Pour each into its own pan and smooth evenly; bake for 12 minutes. Take out of oven and let cool in pans.

Remove paper from back of green cake and place back in the pan; spread evenly with the raspberry preserves (I put the preserves in a small bowl to break it up a little, which makes it easier to spread). Next, remove paper from yellow cake and place on top of green cake; spread evenly with the apricot jam. Then remove paper from red cake and place on top of yellow cake.

Cover the cake with wax paper, tucking it into the sides of the pan. Cover with aluminum foil, place heavy books on top and refrigerate overnight.

Melt your chocolate in double boiler or a pot of water with a smaller pot in it for the chocolate. (You can use the microwave, but be careful not to burn it.)

Put your tricolor cake on a cutting board and spread the chocolate on top and sides and let sit to dry completely.

Using a serrated knife, cut the cake lengthwise and then crosswise to make the cookies (wipe the knife after each slice).

For presentation, place a cookie with chocolate frosting facing out on a pretty cookie dish, making a circle going into the center. At Christmastime, I leave the center space empty and put an artificial poinsettia on top for decoration.

This cookie is always requested by family and friends.

Rugelach

Dough

1 cup (8 oz.) cream cheese, room temperature
1 cup (2 sticks) butter, room temperature
1 ⅔ cups flour

Filling

⅔ cup sugar
1 tbs. ground cinnamon
1 ½ cups finely chopped walnuts
4 tbs. butter, melted
1 egg yolk, beaten with 1 tsp. milk

To prepare dough, beat cream cheese and butter together with a mixer at medium speed until smooth and fluffy. Gradually add half the flour, beating at low speed only until blended. Stir in remaining flour.

Scrape dough onto a lightly floured work surface. Turn to coat with flour and divide into thirds. Shape each portion into a disk and wrap in plastic wrap. Refrigerate overnight.

Preheat oven to 350°. Line two large baking sheets with parchment.

To prepare filling, combine sugar, cinnamon, and walnuts.

Roll one portion of dough on a lightly floured surface into a 12-inch circle. Brush with one-third of the butter and sprinkle with one-third of the walnut mixture. Cover with wax paper and press filling into dough. Remove wax paper. Cut into 12 triangles. Roll each triangle from its wide edge, and set rolls point side down on a baking sheet, one inch apart. Repeat with remaining dough, butter, and filling.

Brush rolls lightly with egg yolk mixture. Bake about 30 minutes, until pastries are golden brown. Rotate baking sheets top to bottom and front to back during baking to ensure even browning. Transfer to a wire rack to cool.

Makes 36 cookies

Sugar Cookies

1 ½ cups powdered sugar
1 cup (2 sticks) butter, softened
1 egg
1 tsp. vanilla extract
½ tsp. almond extract
2 ½ cups all purpose flour
1 tsp. baking soda
1 tsp.cream of tartar
Granulated sugar

Mix powdered sugar, butter, egg, vanilla and almond extract. Stir in flour, baking soda and cream of tartar. Cover and refrigerate at least 3 hours.

Preheat oven 375 °.

Divide dough in halves. On a lightly floured board roll each half to a 3/16 thickness. With a cookie cutter cut into desired shapes and sprinkle sugar on cookie dough.

Place on a lightly grease cookie sheet and bake until edges are light brown, about 7 to 8 minutes.

For holidays and special occasions, I use a fancy cookie cutter and bake the cookies without the sugar on top. When the cookies are cooled I decorate them with a creamy frosting by writing the names of my guest on the cookie using a long thin wooden skewer and use them for fun place cards.

Creamy Frosting

1 cup powdered sugar
½ tsp. vanilla extract
¼ tsp. salt
1-2 tbs. half and half
Food color

Mix powdered sugar, vanilla and salt beat in half and half until a smooth spreading consistency. In separate bowls add some frosting and stir in the colors you like. Decorate cookies then set aside to dry.

Cheesecakes

Almond Joy Cheesecake
Deluxe Cheesecake
Lemon Cheesecake
Peanut Butter Cup Cheesecake
Strawberry Cheesecake
Tiramisu Cheesecake

DO NOT overbeat mixture.

Help prevent cracks in cheesecakes during baking by placing a shallow dish of hot water on bottom rack.

DO NOT open door during baking.

For a perfectly cut cheesecake, first dip a knife in water and dip it for each slice, or hold a piece of dental floss taut between your hands and pull down through the cheesecake, making a clean cut.

Almond Joy Cheesecake

1 ½ cups graham cracker crumbs
3 cups lightly toasted coconut flakes
2 ½ cups lightly toasted sliced almonds
1 ¼ cup sugar
1 stick melted butter
4 8-oz. pkgs. cream cheese, softened
4 large eggs
1 tbs. coconut extract
1 cup chocolate chips
¾ cup heavy cream
½ tsp. vanilla extract

Preheat oven to 350°.

Wrap a 10-inch spring form pan with aluminum wrap 2 ⅔ inches high.

For crust, finely grind graham cracker crumbs, 1 ½ cups toasted coconut, ½ cup toasted almonds, and sugar in food processor; add melted butter and pulse until moistened. Press on bottom and 1 inch up sides of pan; bake 10–12 minutes and cool. Reduce oven to 325°.

For filling, with mixer, beat cream cheese and sugar until smooth; add eggs one at a time and beat. Mix in 1 cup of coconut and coconut extract; fold in 1 cup toasted almonds. Pour into baked cake crust and bake for 1 hour and 15 minutes or until set. Cool completely on wire rack.

For the frosting, combine the heavy cream, chocolate chips, and vanilla extract in a small pot, and heat until it becomes smooth and creamy. Cool till thick but still pourable.

Open side of spring form pan and slide cheesecake onto a wire rack. Place the rack over a cookie sheet and pour your frosting over cake;

smooth evenly with a spatula or knife, covering the sides as well. Slant the cake a little and sprinkle the rest of the toasted almonds up the sides. Sprinkle the rest of the coconut on edges and top of cake.

Chill until completely set before serving.

Deluxe Cheesecake

¾ cup (1 ½ sticks) butter, softened
1 ¼ cup all-purpose flour plus 3 tbs.
2 cups sugar
3 egg yolks
grated peel of 2 small lemons
5 8 oz. packages cream cheese, softened
5 eggs
¼ cup milk

Begin preparing this early in the day or a day ahead.

In a small bowl, with mixer at low speed, beat butter. Add 1 ¼ cups flour, ¼ cup sugar, 1 egg yolk, and one half of grated lemon peel until well mixed. Shape dough into a ball and wrap with plastic wrap; refrigerate 1 hour.

Preheat oven to 400°.

Press one-third of dough into bottom of a 10 × 2 ½ inch spring form pan. Bake 8 minutes; cool.

Turn oven to 475°.

In large bowl, with mixer at medium speed, beat cream cheese just until smooth; slowly beat in 1 ¾ cups sugar. With mixer at low speed, beat in eggs, milk, 3 tbs. flour, remaining 2 egg yolks, and remaining lemon peel. With mixer at medium speed, beat mixture 5 minutes.

Press remaining two-thirds of dough around side of pan to within 1 inch of top; do not bake. Pour cream cheese mixture into pan; bake 12 minutes.

Turn oven control to 300°. Bake 35 minutes longer. Turn off oven; let cheesecake remain in oven 30 minutes. Remove; cool in pan on wire rack. Refrigerate cheesecake at least 4 hours or until well chilled.

To serve, carefully remove cake from pan.

Makes 20 servings

Any canned fruit topping will work on top of this cake or just sprinkle with confectioners' sugar.

Lemon Cheesecake

Crust

    18 gingersnap cookies
    3 tbs. butter, melted

Filling

    4 8-oz. pkgs. cream cheese, softened
    1 ½ cups sugar
    2 tbs. cornstarch
    4 large eggs, at room temperature
    2 tbs. grated lemon zest
    ½ cup lemon juice

Topping

    16 oz. sour cream
    ½ cup sugar
    liquid food color

Garnish

    whipped cream
    quartered lemon slices

Preheat oven to 325°.

Coat an 8 × 3-inch spring form pan with nonstick spray.

Crust

Break cookies into a food processor. Add butter; pulse until fine crumbs form. Press over bottom of prepared pan; freeze until ready to fill.

Filling

Beat cream cheese, sugar, and cornstarch in a large bowl with mixer on medium speed until smooth. On low speed, beat in eggs, one at a time, just until blended. Beat in lemon zest and juice. Pour over crust.

Place on a sheet of foil in oven. Bake 1 ¼ hours, or until puffed around edges and center still jiggles slightly when shaken. Cool 5 minutes or until filling sinks slightly.

Topping

Stir sour cream and sugar in a small bowl until sugar dissolves; tint pale yellow with food color. Pour over filling; spread to edges.

Bake 5 minutes to set. Remove to a wire rack to cool completely.

Carefully run a thin knife around edge of pan to release cake (leave pan sides on). Cover loosely; refrigerate at least 4 hours.

Up to 4 Hours before Serving

Remove pan sides; place cake on a serving plate. Garnish with whipped cream and lemon slices. Refrigerate.

Peanut Butter Cup Cheesecake

Crust

1 cup (about 5 ½ oz.) chocolate wafer cookie crumbs
½ cup (about 2 ½ oz.) roasted unsalted peanuts, coarsely chopped
¼ cup (½ stick) butter
2 tbs. firmly packed light brown sugar
pinch of salt

Filling

4 8-oz. pkg. cream cheese, room temperature
1 ½ cups firmly packed light brown sugar
½ cup creamy peanut butter (do not use old fashioned or freshly ground)
1 tsp. vanilla extract
4 large eggs
¼ cup whipping cream
2 ½ cups (about 10 oz.) ¾-in. pieces Reese's Peanut Butter Cups

Topping

2 cups sour cream
¼ cup sugar
1 tsp. vanilla extract

Position rack in center of oven and preheat to 350°.

Crust

Butter a 9-inch diameter spring form pan with 2 ¾ inch high sides; mix chocolate cookie crumbs, chopped peanuts, melted butter, brown sugar, and pinch of salt in bowl until well combined. Press mixture evenly onto bottom and ½ inch up sides of pan. Bake until crust is set, about 8 minutes. Cool in pan on rack.

Reduce oven temperature to 325°.

Filling

Using an electric mixer, mix at room temperature cream cheese and brown sugar in large bowl until smooth. Add peanut butter and vanilla extract and beat just until blended. Add eggs, one at a time, beating just until blended after each addition. Add whipping cream and beat until smooth. Stir in peanut butter cup pieces.

Pour filling into crust. Bake until sides of cake are set but center still moves slightly, about 55 minutes. Cool cake in pan on rack 10 minutes.

Topping

Blend sour cream, sugar, and vanilla extract in medium bowl. Carefully spoon topping over cheesecake. Return cheesecake to oven and bake 5 minutes.

Cool cheesecake in pan on rack. Run small sharp knife around edge of cheesecake to loosen. Cover and refrigerate overnight. (Can be prepared up to three days ahead. Keep refrigerated.)

Release pan sides. Let stand 20 minutes at room temperature before serving.

Makes 10 servings

Strawberry Cheesecake

Crust

1 9-oz. pkg. Stella D'oro Almond Delight cookies
3 tbs. butter, melted

Filling

4 8-oz. pkgs. cream cheese
1 ¼ cups sugar
1 tbs. cornstarch
4 large eggs, room temperature
8 oz. (scant 1 cup) sour cream
1 tsp. vanilla extract
½ tsp. almond extract
1 cup seedless strawberry jam

Garnish

2 pt. strawberries, bottoms sliced evenly

Heat oven to 325° Coat a 9 × 3-inch spring form pan with nonstick cooking spray.

Crust

Break up cookies in a food processor. Add butter; pulse until fine crumbs form. Press over bottom of prepared pan and freeze until ready to fill.

Beat cream cheese, sugar, and cornstarch in a large bowl with mixer on medium speed until smooth. On low speed, beat eggs, one at a time, just until blended. Add sour cream, vanilla extract, and almond extract; beat just until combined.

Take crust out of freezer and pour one-third of the batter (about 2 cups) into pan; spread evenly. Dot with ¼ cup jam. Spoon on half of the remaining batter (2 cups); gently spread evenly. Dot with ¼ cup jam. Spoon on rest of batter and spread.

Bake 45 minutes or until cake puffs slightly around edges and center still jiggles slightly when shaken. Turn off oven (leave door closed); leave cake in oven 45 minutes.

Carefully run a thin knife around the edge of the pan to release cake (leave on pan sides). Cool completely on a wire rack. Cover and refrigerate at least 4 hours.

Up to 3 hours before Serving

Arrange strawberries, points up, on top of cake. Heat the remaining ½ cup jam in microwave or in a small pan over low heat until melted. Stir until smooth. Spoon over berries; refrigerate to set jam.

Tiramisu Cheesecake

¾ cup strong coffee (reserve 2 tbs.)
1 ¼ cups plus 2 tbs. sugar
1 tbs. Kahlua (coffee flavor liqueur)
1 ½ pkg. (7 oz. each) imported Italian savoiardi ladyfingers (see note)
3 8-oz. pkgs. cream cheese
1 tbs. cornstarch
3 large eggs, at room temperature
8 oz. mascarpone cheese
1 oz. bittersweet chocolate, grated

Garnish: unsweetened cocoa powder and chocolate curls (directions follow)

Remove bottom of a 9 × 3-inch spring form pan; wrap bottom with plastic wrap.

Stir coffee, 2 tbs. sugar, and the Kahlua in a shallow bowl until sugar dissolves. Set half of the ladyfingers aside. For each of the remaining ladyfingers, quickly dip one side into coffee mixture and place wet side up on pan bottom to cover, cutting ladyfingers as needed to fit. Freeze about 15 minutes until firm. Lift plastic wrap, with ladyfingers, off pan bottom and place on a flat plate in freezer.

Preheat oven to 325°.

Reassemble the spring form pan and coat with nonstick spray.

Quickly dip one side of reserved ladyfingers into coffee mixture; place wet side up on pan bottom to cover. Cut ladyfingers to fit and press to fill spaces. Freeze until ready to fill.

Beat cream cheese, 1 ¼ cups sugar, and the cornstarch in a large bowl with mixer on medium speed until smooth. On low speed, beat in eggs, one at a time, just until blended. Beat in mascarpone and reserved 2 tbs. coffee. Pour half the batter (3 cups) into pan and spread evenly. Top with ladyfinger layer from freezer; sprinkle with grated chocolate. Spoon on remaining batter and spread evenly.

Bake 45 minutes or until center still jiggles slightly when shaken. (Air bubbles may form on surface; they'll sink as cake cools.) Turn off oven (leave door closed); leave cake in oven another 45 minutes.

Carefully run a thin knife around the edge of pan to release the cake (leave the pan sides on); cool completely on a wire rack. Cover loosely; refrigerate at least 4 hours, preferably one day for best flavor.

To Serve

Remove pan sides; place cake on a serving plate. Dust with cocoa; top with chocolate curls.

Chocolate Curls

Melt 4 oz. semisweet baking chocolate with 1 tsp. vegetable shortening. Pour into a foil-lined mini loaf pan or sturdy 3 ½ × 2 × 11-inch pan made with layers of foil, and let set at room temperature. Remove the foil and pull a swivel blade vegetable peeler down each length of bar. Refrigerate curls until ready to use.

Note

Imported Italian savoiardi ladyfingers are crisp and longer than the familiar soft sponge cake variety.

Pies and More

The Best Apple Pie
Peach Parfait Pie
Strawberry Pie

Cream Puffs
Date and Nut Bread
Devil Dogs
Flower Pot
Raisin Tarts
Sfingi

When making pie crust, make sure all ingredients are cool.

When making decorative pie edges, use a spoon for a scalloped edge or a fork to make crosshatched or herringbone patterns.

The Best Apple Pie

6 or 7 golden delicious apples, peeled, cored and cut into slices
1 ¼ cup toffee bits or almond brickle chips
⅓ cup sugar
1 tbs. cornstarch
⅛ tsp. salt
11 tbs. butter (1 stick and 3 tbs.) softened
1 ½ cup flour
⅓ cup firmly packed light brown sugar
1 prepared deep-dish pie crust

Preheat oven to 400°.

Carmel Streusel Topping

Combine 9 tbs. butter, flour, brown sugar, and ½ cup toffee bits. Form into two balls and refrigerate.

Filling

In your bowl with sliced apples, add ¾ cup toffee bits, ⅓ cup sugar, cornstarch, salt and toss until all blended. Spoon this mixture into the pie crust and dot with the remaining 2 tbs. butter.

Break the chilled topping into pieces over the apples.

Bake for 20 minutes, the loosely cover the pie with an aluminum foil tent with a hole in the center for air. Bake for 1 hour or until bubbly and crust is golden brown.

This pie is luscious.

Peach Parfait Pie

    1 large can sliced peaches, drained
    1 ¼ cup boiled water
    1 pkg. orange gelatin
    ¼ tsp. almond extract
    1 pint vanilla ice cream
    1 deep-dish pie crust
    canned or fresh whipped cream for topping

Bake pie crust according to directions on package and set aside.

In a bowl, pour the hot water over the orange gelatin and ice cream, and stir to melt. Add extract and fold in sliced peaches; refrigerate. Every 15 minutes stir until thickened. Pour the mixture into your pie shell and refrigerate until set. Serve with a dollop of cream.

Strawberry Pie

    1 ¼ cups graham cracker crumbs
    ¼ cup sugar
    6 tbs. melted butter
    10 oz. frozen strawberries in syrup, thawed
    30 marshmallows (NOT JET-PUFFED)
    1 cup sour cream
    3 oz. cream cheese, softened
    1 tsp. vanilla extract
    A dash salt

Preheat oven to 350°.

In bowl, mix graham cracker crumbs, sugar, and melted butter. Using the back of a spoon, press firmly on bottom and sides of a 9-inch pie plate and bake for 6–8 minutes, Set aside to chill.

In a larger bowl, beat cream cheese, sour cream, vanilla extract, and salt until smooth.

In a medium pot, combine strawberries and marshmallows over medium heat until marshmallows have melted; pour into cream cheese mixture and mix well. Pour into crust and refrigerate for 4 hours or more until set.

When I make this pie, I always make two because everyone always requests a second piece. Serve with a dollop of cream.

Cream Puffs

Of all my desserts the cream puffs are the most asked for and have become my signature dessert.

> 1 stick butter
> 1 cup water
> A pinch salt
> 1 cup flour
> 4 eggs
> 1 pkg. (3 ½ oz.) cook and serve vanilla pudding
> 1 ½ cups milk
> 1 pint heavy cream

Cook vanilla pudding using 1 ½ cup milk until it comes to a full bubbling boil; transfer into a bowl and cover top with a piece of plastic wrap to prevent a skin from forming on pudding. Refrigerate until set. (I make this the day before.)

Preheat oven to 400°.

In a medium pot add water, butter, and salt; just as it starts to boil, add the flour and stir very fast to bring it all together into a ball, continue cooking over medium heat just for a minute to cook off the raw flour.

Take off stove and add one egg at a time, mixing well after each addition.

On an ungreased cookie sheet, place 1 full tablespoon of batter, and with spoon, make sure it's a nice round shape. Bake for 40 minutes. Let puffs cool before you fill them.

Whip your cream to a stiff stage and fold in your pudding.

Slice the top off the puff; take the center out and fill with cream mixture.

Presentation

Sprinkle confectioners' sugar on them. You can also dip the tops into melted chocolate; let set and serve on a pretty dish.

Date and Nut Bread

    1 cup boiled water
    1 ½ tsp. baking soda
    1 ½ cup dates, cut in half
    2 tbs. butter
    2 eggs
    1 cup sugar
    1 tsp. vanilla extract
    2 cups flour
    1 cup chopped walnuts

Preheat oven to 325°.

In a bowl, combine boiled water, baking soda, dates, and butter, and set aside until cooled.

In a larger bowl, beat eggs, sugar, and vanilla until well blended; stir in flour alternating with the fruit mixture until all incorporated. Add nuts and blend.

Pour mixture into a well-greased loaf pan, lined with wax paper on bottom only, and bake for 1 hour or until toothpick inserted in center comes out clean. Cool on a rack and remove from pan. Remove wax paper from bottom, slice, and serve. Serve with cream cheese and jams.

Devil Dogs

Cookies

    2 cups flour
    1 cup sugar
    ½ cup cocoa
    ½ tsp. salt
    ½ tsp. baking powder
    ½ tsp. baking soda
    ½ cup butter, softened
    1 cup milk
    ½ tsp. vanilla extract
    1 egg

Filling

    ½ cup butter, softened
    3 ½ oz. marshmallow cream
    2 cups confectioners' sugar
    4 tsp. milk
    1 tsp. vanilla extract

Preheat oven to 375°.

For cookies, sift flour, sugar, cocoa, salt, baking powder, and baking soda into a bowl; to this add ½ cup butter, milk, vanilla extract, and egg and blend.

Drop by level teaspoonfuls onto greased cookie sheet and bake for 5–7 minutes. Let cool.

For the filling, beat together all filling ingredients until smooth and creamy.

Frost one cookie and cover with another cookie. (I frost half the cookies before I put on tops so I can be sure I have enough filling for the entire batch.) Wrap each cookie in plastic wrap to store or freeze.

Flower Pot

20 oz. bag of Oreo cookies, crushed
1 8-oz. pkg. cream cheese, softened
½ cup butter
2 (3 ½-oz.) boxes instant vanilla pudding
4 cups milk
12 oz. whipped heavy cream
1 cup confectioners sugar

Make pudding according to directions on box and refrigerate until set. Whip cream to very stiff peaks and set aside, when pudding is ready, fold into the heavy cream.

In a larger bowl, cream softened cream cheese and butter together until blended; add pudding and cream mixture and confectioners' sugar, and mix until smooth and creamy.

Using a plastic flower pot lined with plastic wrap, make a layer with your crushed Oreo cookies, followed by a layer of pudding mixture. Continue with layers until you reach top; end with a layer of Oreos.

Cover with plastic wrap and foil and refrigerate overnight.

Presentation

Remove the wraps and stick some artificial flowers in center and serve. The first time I made this I also had gummy worms sticking out of the "dirt."

You can decorate it for any occasion: at Christmas I use artificial poinsettias; for baby showers I use pink or blue flowers with some decorations. For bigger parties I make a triple batch and use a window box pot. What a great presentation that makes. Enjoy this fun dessert.

Raisin Tarts

1 cup of raisins, soaked in hot water to soften and plump
2 tbs. butter, softened
1 scant cup light brown sugar
2 eggs
Pinch of salt
6 tbs. water
1 tsp. vanilla extract
½ cup chopped walnuts
1 box of pie crust mix

Preheat oven to 425°.

In a bowl, add pie crust mix and 4 tbs. cold water, and mix to blend (do not overwork or it will be tough). On a floured surface, roll dough out and cut out twelve 3 ½ circles; place in greased muffin pan.

In bowl, cream butter and brown sugar, add 2 eggs and salt, and beat a few minutes. Stir in 2 remaining tbs. water and vanilla extract. Drain the raisins and add to mixture; blend.

Fill your tarts with mixture and sprinkle walnuts on top. Bake for 30 minutes or till golden brown. Remove from oven; take tarts out of pan and place on a rack to cool.

Sfingi

1 lb. ricotta
2 eggs
½ tsp. baking powder
5 tsp. sugar
1 cup flour more as needed
6 cups of oil

Preheat fryer or pot of oil to 360°.

Mix all ingredients in a bowl and add flour until mixture is fluffy and sticky.

Drop full tablespoons of dough into oil. They will pop up to top, but just keep pushing them back down into oil. Flip over when they are a deep golden brown; scoop out and let drain on rack to cool. Transfer them to a platter and sprinkle with confectioners' sugar.

Candy

Chocolate Covered Pretzels
Peanut Clusters
Raisin and Coconut Clusters
Turtles
Christmas Wreaths with Berries

Use a double boiler when melting chocolate to prevent from scorching. A slow cooker on the lowest setting also works when melting a large amount of chocolate.

I also use the microwave; put chocolate in bowl and start with 2 minutes, stopping frequently to stir. Be careful because I have burnt a lot of chocolate doing that extra 20 seconds. Consistency should be smooth and creamy. If your chocolate isn't quite where you want it to be, let it stand for a brief time; chances are the heat of the rest of the chocolate will be enough to melt and smooth out any little lumps.

When I make a lot of candy, I put a sheet of wax paper in between layers of candy to store until I'm ready to party.

These candies are so simple to make and look great on your holiday table.

Chocolate Covered Pretzels

1 lb. melted milk chocolate
1 lb. melted white chocolate
pretzel logs

Once first chocolate is melted, lay a long piece of waxed paper on table and pour some chocolate in a mug. Dip a pretzel log in halfway; let all excess chocolate drip off and place on the waxed paper.

When chocolate has set completely, melt the second chocolate and dip the other end of pretzel in. Again lay on the waxed paper until set.

If you don't want it two shades, just use the flavor of your choice. When dried, lift and place in covered container until ready to serve.

Peanut Clusters

1 lb. melted chocolate
1 large jar of unsalted dry peanuts

In the bowl of melted chocolate, add ¾ of the nuts and stir to coat, keep adding nuts as long as there is enough chocolate to coat. Drop a full tablespoon of mixture on a sheet of waxed paper and let dry. When set, lift and place in a covered container until ready to serve.

Raisin and Coconut Clusters

    1 lb. melted chocolate
    1 bag flaked coconut
    1 box of raisins

In the bowl of melted chocolate, stir coconut and raisins to coat. Spoon full tablespoons of mixture on waxed paper and let cool to set. When set, lift and place in covered container until ready to serve.

Turtles

1 unopened can sweetened condensed milk, boiled for 2 hours and chilled (when opened it looks like caramel)
1 lb. chocolate, melted
1 bag of shelled pecans

Place a long piece of waxed paper on table. Spoon teaspoonfuls of chocolate on paper; with back of spoon make them into even circles. Place 2 pecans on circles, spoon some caramel over top and cover with chocolate to cover the cluster.

With back of spoon, go over edges of cluster to seal. Once set, just lift off waxed paper. Keep in covered containers until ready to serve.

Christmas Wreaths with Berries

1 lb. white chocolate, melted
1 bag of flaked coconut
1 container of cinnamon red hot candy for decoration

To melted chocolate, add coconut to make a thick consistency. Put a dollop of mixture on waxed paper. With back of spoon, working from the center, form into the shape of a wreath, leaving nothing in center. Place 3 red hot candies in cluster on bottom of wreath to look like berries.

Dips and That

Cheddar Cheese and Beer Dip
Layered Taco Dip
Mushroom Dip
Spinach and Artichoke Dip

Bread and Butter Pickles
Hot Pepper Sauce
Pesto
Reduced Balsamic Vinegar
Roux

Cheddar Cheese and Beer Dip

1 large container of cheddar cheese spread
1 8-oz. pkg. cream cheese, softened
1 can of beer
1 tsp. garlic powder

Combine the cheddar cheese, cream cheese, and garlic powder, and mix well. Add beer a little at a time until you get a thickness that is suitable for dipping. If you wish, you can add more garlic powder.

Layered Taco Dip

16 oz. can of refried beans
8 oz. cream cheese, softened
1 cup mayonnaise
1 tbs. lemon juice
1 pkg. taco seasoning mix
2 bunches of scallions, diced
3 medium tomatoes, diced
2 cups shredded cheddar cheese
1 bag nacho chips

In a bowl combine cream cheese, mayonnaise, lemon juice, and taco seasoning mix.

On a large platter spread the refried beans to within two inches of the edge of the platter. Follow this with the cream cheese mixture. Next, layer diced scallions and then diced tomatoes. Top with shredded cheddar cheese as the final layer.

Place the nacho chips along the edge of the platter.

Mushroom Dip

1 large onion chopped fine
2 tbs. butter
2 tbs. lemon juice, fresh or bottled
2 14-oz. cans of sliced mushrooms with one can drained
1 cup plain bread crumbs
1 15-oz. pkg. shredded cheddar cheese

Preheat oven to 350 degrees

In a 2 qt. sauce pan melt butter, add onions and sauté over medium high heat until soft but translucent, add mushrooms and lemon juice. Bring the mixture to a boil, then lower heat and simmer for 5 minutes.

In a large bowl add the mushroom mixture, the bread crumbs and stir to blend completely.

In an oven proof bowl with a cover, add half of the mushroom mixture, sprinkle a layer of the cheddar cheese. Add the remaining mushroom mixture, followed with remaining cheddar cheese.

Cover and place in oven. Bake until the cheese is melted and bubbly. Serve with assorted crackers.

Note: before cooking I dice the mushrooms to make the finished dish easier to scoop onto a cracker.

Another variation: this dip can also be made with clams in place of the mushrooms or a combination of both to equal 2 cans.

Spinach and Artichoke Dip

½ cup shallots, minced
2 10-oz. pkgs. chopped frozen spinach, thawed and drained
4 cloves fresh garlic, minced
4 tbs. butter
2 8-oz. cans quartered artichoke hearts, drained
2 cups heavy cream
4 oz. garlic herb cheese spread
1 tsp. kosher salt
½ tsp. white pepper
¼ cup grated Parmesan cheese

In a large frying pan, sauté shallots and garlic in butter over medium heat. Add well-drained spinach and artichokes and cook on low to heat briefly.

Add cream, garlic, herb cheese, salt, and pepper. Simmer until cheese is melted and mixture is blended.

Remove from heat, and fold in the grated Parmesan cheese.

Place in heatproof crock pot or ramekin.

Serve warm with tortilla chips, pita chips, or your favorite crackers. May be made ahead of time and gently reheated.

Bread and Butter Pickles

    2 cups sugar
    2 cups cider vinegar
    3 tbs. kosher salt
    2 tbs. yellow mustard seeds
    1 tsp dry mustard powder
    1 tsp. dry turmeric
    1 tsp. hot red pepper flakes
    ½ tsp. celery seeds
    2 ½ lbs. pickling cucumbers (about 12), cut into ¼-in. slices
    2 medium onions, sliced

In a large pot, bring all ingredients except cucumbers and onions to a boil, stirring occasionally until sugar is dissolved. Add the cucumbers and onions; stir over high heat one minute. Remove from heat.

With a slotted spoon, transfer cucumbers and onions to four clean pint jars. Pour pickling liquid over pickles to cover. Cover loosely with lids and let cool. Tighten lids; refrigerate and use within two weeks.

Hot Pepper Sauce

My husband loves hot and spicy food, but I shy away from the really hot stuff. What he didn't like was the terrible taste of store-bought sauces, which were so hot that they masked the flavor of the food you put it on. One day, after reading a recipe from one of my cookbooks, he made a variation of this hot sauce. What is perfect about this sauce is that you can make it as hot or as mild as you like just by using different kinds of hot peppers, from the very hot habanera to the mild Anaheim.

    20 assorted hot peppers
    1 sweet red bell pepper
    1 tbs. cayenne pepper
    3 tbs. hot red pepper flakes
    ½ tsp. kosher salt
    1 tbs. garlic powder
    vegetable oil

When working with hot peppers, always wear gloves for protection from the oil inside the pepper.

Remove stems from peppers. Process all the ingredients except for the oil in a food processor until the peppers are cut into a very fine dice.

Put peppers into a large pot; add enough oil to cover and then bring to a boil over high heat. Let it boil for a minute, stirring so nothing sticks to the bottom; lower the heat to simmer and cook for another 5 minutes, stirring occasionally.

Remove from heat and let cool. When cool, pour everything into a glass jar. Cover.

The sauce is best after seven days. You can either let it stay on the counter or put it in the refrigerator.

You can use this sauce on just about anything, but we like it best on top of pasta with red sauce.

Pesto

2 cups fresh basil
2 cloves garlic, chopped
¼ cup toasted pine nuts
⅔ cup oil
kosher salt to taste
½ cup grated Romano cheese

Put all ingredients into a food processor and process until smooth.

Can be tossed with cooked pasta or spread on toasted bread or homemade mozzarella.

Reduced Balsamic Vinegar

2 cups balsamic vinegar
2 tbs. sugar

Bring balsamic vinegar and sugar to a boil. Reduce heat and simmer until reduced by half and a syrupy consistency.

Roux

A roux is a thickening agent just like cornstarch. It is usually made from equal amounts of fat and flour with the best being flour and butter. A roux is started by melting butter or other fat, adding flour, and cooking the two together over low heat while whisking or stirring constantly to prevent burning. There are three types of roux: white, blond, and brown. White roux, used to make traditional white sauce, should be cooked just until the butter and flour are evenly incorporated and smooth and should be removed before the roux begins to darken, 3–5 minutes. Blond roux, used in cream soups, cooks until it turns an ivory color, 6–7 minutes. Brown roux, mainly used in Cajun and Creole cooking, is cooked 8–15 minutes. Remember, the longer you cook a roux, the less it will thicken.

2 tbs. butter
2 tbs. flour

In a pot melt 2 tbs. butter and add 2 tbs. flour; blend together until smooth (I use the back of my spoon for this). Stir over medium heat a few minutes to cook off the raw flour; slowly add 2 cups of liquid (milk for creamed foods, stock for gravies). Stir constantly to blend the flour into the liquid and cook until it has thickened.

Measurements, Oven Conversions, and Helpful Hints

The next few pages will be measurements, conversions for cooking temperatures, and many helpful hints.

Measurements

A pinch	⅛ teaspoon or less
3 teaspoons	1 tablespoon
4 tablespoons	¼ cup
8 tablespoons	½ cup
12 tablespoons	¾ cup
16 tablespoons	1 cup
8 fluid ounces	1 cup
2 cups	1 pint
4 cups	1 quart
4 quarts	1 gallon
16 ounces	1 pound
32 ounces	1 quart

C to F Conversion

120 C	250 F
140 C	275 F
150 C	300 F
160 C	325 F
180 C	350 F
190 C	375 F
200 C	400 F
220 C	425 F
230 C	450 F

1 cup = 8 fl. oz. = 16 tbsp.= 48 tsp. = 237 ml
¾ cup = 6 fl. oz. = 12 tbsp.= 36 tsp. = 177 ml
⅔ cup = 5 ⅓ fl. oz. = 10 ⅔ tbsp. = 32 tsp. = 158 ml
½ cup = 4 fl. oz. = 8 tbsp. = 24 tsp. = 118 ml
⅓ cup = 2 ⅔ fl. oz. = 5 ⅓ tbsp. = 16 tsp. = 79 ml
¼ cup = 2 fl. oz. = 4tbsp. = 12 tsp. = 59 ml
⅛ cup = 1 fl. oz. = 2 tbsp. = 6 tsp. = 30 ml
1 tbsp. = 3 tsp. = 15 ml

Roasting Chart

Meats	Weight	Time	Temperature (°F)
Poultry			
Chicken	Whole (3–4 lbs.)	1 ¼ -1 ½ hrs.	350
	5–7 lbs.	2–2 ¼ hrs.	350
Turkey, unstuffed	12–18 lbs.	3–4 ½ hrs.	325
	19–24 lbs.	4 ½–5 hrs.	325
Pork			
Ham, fully cooked	7–8 lbs.	18–25 min./lb.	325
bone in	14–16 lbs.	15–18 min./lb.	325
Pork loin roast	2–5 lbs.	20–25 min./lb.	350
Pork ribs	2–4 lbs.	1 ½–2 hrs.	350
Beef			
Rib roast	4–8 lbs.	27–38 min,/lb.	325
Eye round roast	2–3 lbs.	20–22 min./lb.	325
Tenderloin (whole)	4–6 lbs.	45–60 min.	425

Food Storage Guidelines

	Refrigerator 35–40 °	Freezer 0 or lower
Fresh Meats		
Beef roast and steaks	3–4 days	6–12 months
Beef, ground	1–2 days	3–4 months
Veal	1–2 days	4–6 months
Pork chops	2–3 days	4–6 months
Pork roast	3–5 days	4–8 months
Pork sausage	1–2 days	1–2 months
Bacon	2 weeks	3 months
Ham, whole	1 week	1–2 months
Chicken and turkey	1–2 days	12 months
Fish	1–2 days	3–6 months

Eggs

	Raw	4–5 weeks
	Hard-boiled	5 days

Dairy

Cottage cheese	1 week	2 weeks
Sour cream	2 weeks	
Yogurt	2 weeks	
Hard cheese	3–4 months	6 months
Processed cheese	1 month	6 months
Ice cream		2 months
Margarine and butter	2–4 weeks	9 months
Milk	8–20 days	

Other

Mustard	6–8 months	12 months
Mayonnaise	12 months	
Bread	1–2 weeks	3 months
Frozen vegetables		8 months
Frozen fruit		1 year
Fruit juice concentrate	6 days	1 year

Pasta Cooking Time

I wanted making pasta to be easy for you, so I went to the supermarket and read all the following pasta boxes.

I always taste for doneness anyway and usually leave it a little longer, but these are good starting guidelines.

Angel Hair: 1–2 min.
Cannelloni: 7–9 min.
Fettuccine: 6–8 min.
Lasagna: 10–12 min.
Linguine: 7–9 min.
Macaroni (variety): 8–10 min.
Manicotti: 7–9 min.
Ravioli: 7–9 min.

Rigatoni: 10–12 min.
Rotelle: 8–10 min.
Spaghetti: 10–12 min.
Tubettini (great for soup): 5–7 min.
Tortellini: 10–12 min.
Vermicelli: 4–6 min.
Ziti: 10–12 min.

Helpful Hints

Over the years of reading cookbooks and watching cooking shows, and from my own experiences, I have collected a few helpful hints I want to share with you.

- When making hors d'oeuvres, to keep the cheeses moist until serving them, cover the platter with a damp paper towel and then loosely with plastic wrap. Store your platter on bottom shelf in refrigerator where the temperature is more even.
- Always bring your cheeses to room temperature before serving. The flavors will be more intense.
- To make your dips a little different, cut a red, green, and yellow pepper in half and clean out the seeds and ribs. Fill the pepper halves with your dips.
- To make fancy butter pats, soften 1 stick of butter to room temperature and put in a pastry bag with a fancy tip (rosette or ribbon). Squeeze the butter onto a baking or cookie sheet and refrigerate until set.
- Freeze some grapes; you can use them for ice cubes.
- Don't panic if you get a last-minute guest. If you have tomatoes, pasta, garlic, and grated cheese in the house, you can get a meal together. Make a salad to go along with your pasta, and you're set.
- Always use a large pot when browning meat. If it's too small, the steam from the food will make your meat look grayish. A large pot gives the meat room to breathe.
- Use plenty of water when making your pasta and keep it at

- a heavy boil. The pasta needs to move while cooking. This also prevents it from sticking.
- When making pasta, don't rinse after cooking. Your sauce will stick to your pasta better and you'll retain the nutrients.
- Always defrost your meats in the refrigerator. Defrosting in a microwave will partially cook it and can leave you with a dried piece of meat.
- To prevent a roast from sticking on bottom of pan, place a few stalks of celery under the meat. This can be used for chicken and turkey as well.
- Turkey is a great source of protein because it is very low in fat. It's high in B vitamins, which are good for the body for a variety of reasons, and the amino acid tryptophan, which helps in restful sleep. This makes turkey a great late night snack.
- The best way to defrost a turkey is in a shallow pan in the refrigerator in its original packaging. Allow 24 hours for every 5 lbs. of turkey.
- Because of the risk of food poisoning, it is no longer advised to stuff a turkey. But if you enjoy it best that way, then make sure your stuffing mixture is completely cooled before you put into turkey. Remove it as soon as possible once cooked, and then let the turkey sit for 20 minutes before carving. For year-round answers to questions on cooking turkey, call 1-800-BUTTERBALL. Also for more recipes and free coupons, try www.butterball.com.
- When sautéing or frying, heat pan before adding butter or oil to prevent sticking.
- Sprinkling a little salt in pan before frying keeps the oil from splattering and makes clean up a little easier.
- For fluffy baked potatoes, pierce the potato with a fork in several spots; this will allow the steam to escape.
- When making sauces or soups, if you put in too much salt, just add a peeled raw potato and that should do the trick.
- Save your leftover garlic bread. Freeze and later use as bread crumbs for chicken or chops for added flavor.

- An easy way to separate eggs is to crack them into a funnel. The white will slide out leaving the yolk in funnel.
- If you like using fresh herbs better, then a good way to keep any you didn't use for a recipe from going bad is to chop, add a little water, and place in ice cube tray and freeze. When you next need that herb, just pop out a cube. Or loosely wrap them in a damp paper towel and store in a plastic bag in the vegetable crisper.
- Wrap celery in aluminum foil and store in the vegetable crisper; it will last for weeks and weeks. When storing lettuce, remove the center core, wrap in paper towels, and place in a Ziploc bag or air tight container.
- Line your vegetable drawer with paper towels to absorb excess moisture.
- To prevent your plastic bowls from getting food stains, spray them first with a cooking spray before pouring in sauces.

I hope this has been a helpful chapter.

Well, my new friends, I must say it has been with excitement and pleasure to bring this dream of mine together for you. I hope you'll try and enjoy these recipes as much as our family has. Please keep me posted on your favorites. Be sure to check the Web page; I'll be posting new ideas for theme parties and favors as well as lots of pictures.

And remember to always follow that dream in your heart.

Love Debbie ♥

Thank You, Mom and Daddy
Always and Forever in my Heart

Index